GOOD WORK

BRUCE
HIEBERT

GOOD
WORK

How to
Live Your Values in
the Workplace

Northstone

Editor: Michael Schwartzentruber
Cover and interior design: Margaret Kyle
Cover artwork: "The Carousel," Marion Stuck
Consulting art director: Robert MacDonald

Northstone Publishing Inc. is an employee-owned company, committed to caring for
the environment and all creation. Northstone recycles, reuses and composts, and encourages readers
to do the same. Resources are printed on recycled paper and more environmentally friendly
groundwood papers (newsprint), whenever possible. The trees used are replaced through donations
to the Scoutrees For Canada Program. Ten percent of all profit is donated to charitable organizations.

Canadian Cataloguing in Publication Data
Hiebert, Bruce.
Good work
ISBN 1-896836-06-2
1. Work. – Psychological aspects. 2. Self-actualization
(Psychology) 3. Conduct of life I. Title.
HD4905.H53 1997   158.7   C97-910445-9

Published by
Northstone Publishing Inc., Kelowna, British Columbia

Printing
9 8 7 6 5 4 3 2 1

Printed in Canada by
Transcontinental Printing Inc.,
Peterborough, Ontario

To the volunteers and staff
of the Mennonite Central Committee,
good workers.

Acknowledgments

This book is the product of a community too large to thank individually, but special recognition needs to go to a few. The board and staff of Mennonite Central Committee British Columbia, especially Waldo Neufeld, supported this project in its preliminary stages. Dave Hubert and Jack Klassen, of Mennonite Central Committee Canada, pushed me to start putting this material on paper. Along the way, the staff and members of Vancouver's Workplace Ministry put up with my questions and offered support, especially Greg Huynh, David Hughes, Conrad Guelke, John Kutchenthal, and Harlene Walker. Eric Wiebe, Henry Hubert, Walter Klaassen and especially Marcus Smucker contributed more than they know. David Cleary and Mike Schwartzentruber of Northstone Publishing Inc. had a big hand in taking the ideas and giving them coherence. Finally, my gracious thanks to Marlene, Katherine, and Gregory for putting up with an absent husband and father.

Contents

1

A Life of Work

Life is work. Not only that, work is changing and therefore life is changing.

Curiously, I did not really become aware of this fact until 1991, when I was involuntarily dumped into the leading edge of the new economy. "Dehired," some call it. "Fired" was more like it. And even though I saw it coming, I was unprepared. It felt as though I had been dropped into a bath of ice water. Surprisingly, the economic shock was not the worst of it. The settlement package was generous. What I felt most was the blow to my identity. I had lost my title. In the space of a day I went from being a "somebody" to being a "nobody." I had lost my social standing. Friends no longer knew what to make of me. I felt frightened and completely alone.

Fortunately, I was not as alone or as badly off as I felt. As I came to grips with the shock and started putting my life back together, I discovered I had a loving family, no immediate financial worries, a network of supportive peers, access to professional counseling (as part of the severance package), and a wealth of interests reflected in my many "non-professional" activities.

My biggest fear, at the time, was that I would not be able to find another job. I was raised in the "old" economy of big employers and long-term jobs. As I understood the rules of that system, being fired represented a huge black mark on my record – a sign of irresponsibility, poor attitudes, and questionable trustworthiness. With that new strike against me, plus a history of esoteric education (two graduate degrees in theology) and a record of short-term employment, I feared that I was out of the game. What future did I have? No respectable employer, I thought, was going to be happy to see me.

As it turned out, I had a good future. As I started looking at my options, I realized that while I had been working, the world had been changing and things were far different than they had been. In fact, from my particular point of view, things were better.

The first thing I noticed was that for the first time in my working career, my work history was no longer a detriment. Until then, the only people I had heard of who changed jobs as often as I had were writers. Now, I found that lots of people were changing jobs, and there was even the beginning of a suspicion that those who stayed in jobs for a long time might not be the best workers. Even better, my problem solving abilities and creativity, which were always troublesome to my rigid past employers, were now being called "entrepreneuring" and becoming prized. Big changes! And I liked them.

So I settled in to the new economy, found a job that continued to keep me at the leading edge of economic and workplace changes (working with those suffering its negative consequences), and started thinking. What got me thinking was that if I, who had studied much and was deeply concerned about what is happening to other people

(15 years in social services related work) had been taken by surprise, then how many other people were being taken by surprise?

Each of us will spend more of our waking hours working, or preparing for work, or recovering from work, than we will spend on any other activity in our whole lives. Yet how many of us spend time reflecting on that fact, or the impact it has on us? I realized that our lack of reflection was leaving us unprepared and vulnerable.

Then the second thing hit me. These changes were not just about work, they were about what it means to be human. The new economy was pushing us to change the way work fits into our lives, and the way our lives fit into our work, and it was doing so in ways which drove to the root of what it means to be human. The changes were not just economic and social, they were also profoundly spiritual.

I must admit, at the outset, that not everyone draws the same conclusions that I do. There is a lot of nostalgia floating in some corners for a way of life which is passing. I do not share that nostalgia. While there was much stability in the old industrial and bureaucratic world, it was (and still is) highly destructive to both people and planet. There is also an excessive technological optimism on the part of some pundits regarding what the future holds. They seem convinced that with enough robots and computers we will achieve heaven on earth. While I am willing to embrace many of the new technologies, realism requires that we acknowledge that there are negative consequences. Some of those consequences are devastating. And finally, there are still a few people who seem not to have faced the ecological fragility of our planet.

It was the combined force of these two "discoveries" – our vulnerability in the face of a changing work world, and the essentially spiritual nature of these changes – that provided the impetus for this book. These insights form the basis of everything that follows.

Spirituality

When I say that the changes that are taking place, that *need* to take place, are essentially spiritual, I mean spirit-centered in the broadest sense, as that which takes us to the heart of what it means to be human and what it means to participate in our society. The spiritual concerns of this book grapple not only with the way things *are*, but with the *why* of things, and the *way* of things. Workplace spirituality engages our identity, our activity, and our relationships. Our work reflects our deepest commitments, our strengths and weaknesses, our hopes and fears. At the same time, it takes us into the social realm where our society functions in relation to the planet as a whole. Our work draws upon the energy and ecology of our planet, and changes it. We work with the very stuff of life, shaping it to fit human desires.

I believe we *live*, spiritually, out of our essence (which includes our core values and beliefs), and that our *essence* is in turn shaped by how we live. Each is shaped and refined by the other, and our work is central to this process of molding. Our work is something that speaks *of us* and *to us*. The things we do as we work say much about what really counts in our lives. And what we *experience* through our work tells us much about what is real and what is illusion in the world around us. Good work, as we shall see, follows the way of the spirit, the way of truth. It is a spiritual journey which takes us to the heart of all things.

The factors that have allowed this new spirituality of work to emerge are not hard to see. For most of human history, up until this last century, our work was determined by the circumstances of our birth. (Usually that meant we farmed.) There was little point talking about work; the only thing we had to look forward to was rest (which explains much of the power behind holy days). The demands of life in that older world did not leave us much time to ask what work meant and how we should do it.

Today, there are at least 20,000 occupational categories in North America with more being added every day. Today, it is not so much that we climb a career ladder, as that we embark upon a career journey. We make our way following aptitude, circumstance, and interest. Today, we can take our work into our own hands. We can choose how we earn our daily bread.

At the same time, idleness afflicts us. Most of us desire to be productive, but that opportunity is withheld from many who want it. Many of us scrabble for whatever work we can find, whether that means we end up being self-employed, under-employed, or part-time employed. And all of us can expect to experience at least brief periods of unemployment.

Other forces driving this change are primarily technological. Computerization and automation, cheap travel and easy telecommunication have probably been the most powerful influences of the last 50 years. Their cumulative impact on human life has been tremendous and the changes they have led to in our work are almost impossible to measure.

So when we talk about the spirituality of work, or of work as a spiritual journey, when we tackle the meaning of work in the space-time we now inhabit, and try to integrate it holistically into our lives, we are forced to think carefully each step of the way. Our situation has changed, but our language and thinking are only slowly catching up.

Wisdom

I find it interesting how words go in and out of fashion. Wisdom is one of those words which has had a tremendous history, and which has recently been rediscovered. In much the same way as the word leadership got lost within the language of management, wisdom got lost in the language of skills. As a culture, we became so obsessed with mastery of skills and technical abilities we stopped asking the question "why" and therefore stopped needing wisdom in order to point us in the right direction. But just as leadership is making a comeback, so also is wisdom. A recent check of the local bookstores indicates that in the self-help, business, and spirituality sections wisdom shows up in the titles in a big way. It points to something which we have neglected in our search for mastery but are now coming back to, as we have accumulated skills but in the process have become solitary specialists, and as knowledge piles up in unusable quantities all around us. In our information-overloaded, high-tech world wisdom has become important once again.

Wisdom is, at its root, the ability to see what is real, what is genuinely significant. I am wise when I can see what is truly happening around me, and know how I should respond to it. Wisdom involves insight into relationships. I am wise in my relationships when I know what those closest to me – partners, friends, lovers, parents, and children – need from their relationship with me, and how I should respond to them for their good as well as mine. When my daughter throws a temper tantrum, not an unusual occurrence for a teenager, I need to be able to see what it represents: hormonal imbalance perhaps, or fatigue, or psychological manipulation, or all of the above. Then I need to be able to see what my appropriate response should be, for her good.

What I discover quite quickly is that wisdom is something fleeting. It is also something learned. The more I attempt to understand, and therefore the more I gain those fleeting glimpses, the more I learn about where and how to look. In my daughter's case, I soon learn what the tone of voice, or the situation, indicates about what is truly going on. I become wise to her ways. Of course, my daughter and my relationship to her grows and changes, so I will have to relearn many lessons as I go along. However, over time, a store of wisdom builds up.

But what does wisdom about work look like? Since wisdom is about finding and having insights into relationships, we must ask, "What are the inner relationships which define work and its connection to the rest of life? What effects does our work have, not just on our paycheques, but on ourselves as people, on those around us, and on the planet itself?" Wisdom will come as we learn to see the real outcomes of our work. When we are wise to our work, we will ask the right questions, see the real relationships, and make the changes necessary to improve our work.

This kind of wisdom is not something we attain quickly and easily. Often it is not until we are dumped out of our work, like I was in 1991, or forced to face the dark side of our work, that we begin to see the connections between our work and who we are as people and communities. Wisdom is usually only found after painful struggle and often reveals as much about ourselves as it does about the object of our concern.

One of the common obstacles to wisdom about work is work itself. We teach a class, lay a row of bricks, complete a report, diaper a child, manage a meeting. And as soon as we have finished, there is another task waiting to be done. There are so many things to do – *important* things, things *other people* are counting on us to do, things we *want* to do. We can work without stopping, and when we *do* stop to rest, the last thing we want to think about is work. The result is that we do a great deal of work while giving very little thought to what it all means.

Also, in too many cases, our work causes pain, and wisdom is something we would rather not have. Wisdom might call for change or confrontation and sometimes that is more than we can cope with. Work cuts through to our identity. Sleepless nights and ulcers notwithstanding, it is sometimes easier to hope that the bad stuff will go away than it is to grow wise to our work and make the changes that come from wisdom.

Responsibility

The way of wisdom is not easy. It takes time and experience, a supportive community, and a willingness to risk. That we cannot stop in our pursuit of wisdom is due to another important word – responsibility. Our work changes the world in little ways every day, and so we have a responsibility to know what we are doing. We cannot ignore the consequences of what we do or deny responsibility because other people set the rules. Every day we work, we make decisions, act in specific ways, and therefore bear responsibility for what we have done. Any decision we make could have been made differently, and any order we carry out could have been interpreted in many ways, or even denied. It is *our* work and it is *our* responsibility.

Our responsibility is not only individual. It is also collective. As we work together we have a collective impact on each other and the planet around us. Decisions made, actions taken, and pathways chosen in our committees, corporations and councils have their consequences. The bad news is that our collective decisions to date have put the planet itself at risk. The good news is that these were *our* decisions and so we can choose to do otherwise in the future.

Joy

There is one more reason for pursuing wisdom about work and that is joy. In work we engage our whole beings, and when it turns out right the experience is deeply satisfying. Work can be extremely joyful. We can, to contradict a bumper sticker, find that "a bad day at work is better than a good day fishing." Work provides the opportunity for creative expression, for productive exploration, for action and positive reaction. We can take care of our families, create a better world, make friends, express our identities, learn, and grow through our work. Work can be a very joyful activity, and wisdom helps us to identify those places where it is already joyful and how we can make it even more joyful.

I find my work very satisfying. I awake in the morning eager to go to work, happy to face the challenges, and sorry at the end of the day to see it end. I enjoy the people with whom I work, treasure the challenges and opportunities of the work, and take pride in my and our accomplishments on the job. My work is a source of tremendous energy. It gives me the strength to take on other challenges, to participate in the life of my community, and to carry on in the face of pain. I find great joy in my work, and while I make no claim to having discovered *the* way of wisdom, I know that working as wisely as I am able is something worth every bit of the effort that has gone into it.

2

Work and Identity

One of the worst things about losing your job is that you always lose so much more than just your job. When I was fired back in 1991, I stepped, almost instantaneously, out of a job and role which I loved and with which I identified, and into an abyss. It was a time of heavy denial – not of my job loss, that I accepted with some relief, but of the effect of this change on my identity. For at least six months, part of me continued to act as if I still had my old job. I behaved in keeping with its norms. I talked to others with the language and as if I had the responsibility which went with my old job. Eventually, to my utter humiliation, friends started commenting on my refusal to step out of the role, though in fact, and this was the *real* source of the humiliation, I had not realized until then that I was still acting out of it.

I know I was not unique in this behavior. I have heard of laid off bankers who continue for months to get dressed in suit and tie, pick up the briefcase, and head downtown, even if only to spend the day at the library. I did nothing that extreme (at least from my point of view!), but I know it took a long time for my "identity" to catch up with the reality of my unemployment.

Why this happens is not hard to see. From the very first time we are asked, as little children, what we want to be when we grow up, we begin to think of ourselves in terms of "our" job. Later, we are pushed through schooling and learning designed to ready us for work. By the time we actually enter the working world, the tendency to identify ourselves with our work is thoroughly engrained. "What do you do?" is the question that most frequently follows "What is your name?" Sometimes it is the *first* question.

Identity is a funny thing for most of us. We name ourselves as businesspeople, teachers, lawyers, nurses, homemakers, garbage collectors, doctors, and writers with an ease completely out of keeping with the complexity of what we are doing in that naming. Each of these addresses us, not "as we really are," but through our role in the workplace.

For those who work with us, the job site may be their only point of contact with us. For them, "who we really are" is often "who we are on the job." We may complain about this (and rightly so sometimes) but should we begin to step outside that role in inappropriate ways (such as when a boss sees him/herself as a potential lover) all sorts of bad things can happen.

Yet this role identity continues even off the job. Our families, even though they do not relate to us on the job (or did not until the recent surge in home based business) are also not immune from identifying us with our work. And our broader community of friends and acquaintances very often makes assumptions about our probable likes and dislikes, intelligence, creativity, lifestyle, social standing, etc., based on the labels we use to describe our work.

For most of us, when all this happens our own sense of identity and worth follows along behind. Some of us fight it, and some of us succeed in breaking out of the molds our work may cast us in, but all of us are affected by our workplace identity.

This whole area of identity concerns me because the spiritual journey we make when we attempt to find and do good work is not one we can hold separate from who we are and what we experience in the workplace. For example, if my work leads to a sense of worthlessness, my spiritual journey becomes dark and empty. (This is one of the central problems caused by unemployment. Idled workers feel worthless and withdraw into themselves.) On the other hand, if I am lucky enough to experience work as an outlet for my creativity, this can have an extremely energizing affect on my spirituality.

But my deeper concern in all this is that the labels we use to define ourselves as workers are simply too superficial. We need to move beyond the common labels which serve mostly to identify professional categories or tasks. (We are doctors, lawyers, teachers, welders, etc.) Our identity in the workplace *is* important, but the central or most important feature of that identity is *not* the specific job we do.

I believe there are *six* archetypal roles we embody and that come alive for us in our work, regardless of the type of work we do. Some of these roles are ancient, some are more recent "inventions," but *all* of them are crucial as part of our self-definition as workers. It is *these* roles and their relationship to good work that we must understand. In fact, I believe that good work springs directly from one of these roles in particular. But I am jumping ahead of myself.

Let us take these roles in turn.

Provider

The oldest and most basic role we play as workers is that of *provider*. The provider is the one who brings the resources necessary for group survival. This role stretches back to our very earliest forebears and can be found among many animals. The parents of many species provide food and shelter for their offspring through their efforts and skill. Among us moderns, this type of behavior is called "making a living."

The role of provider is a highly egalitarian one: both men and women, old and young, can assist with providing the resources needed for survival as a family or group. The role of provider is also viewed and experienced very positively. All communities need providers in order to survive and prosper. Those who provide usually receive positive feedback from the group because their efforts help to make the group healthier and happier. And as a result of this feedback, those who provide usually experience pride and esteem knowing they have done well for the community.

Spiritually, the role of provider reminds us of our fundamental physicality. No *journey* is possible if we do not have the physical resources to make it. No *life* is possible if we do not have the physical resources to live it. As providers, we also learn to recognize and work with one of the fundamental laws of the universe – all things must participate in the cycles of birth, growth, and death. Providers must face the universal truth that the cost of our sustenance usually includes the death of some other living things. As providers, we are involved in the ultimate dramas of life itself.

Unfortunately, the value of this archetype has become obscured by the complexity and insensitivity of our culture. Though we may seek to be *providers*, it is hard in our technological culture to raise this role and celebrate it independent of our modern role as *consumers*.

Too often, we celebrate the provision of resources, not as something achieved in partnership with nature (a sign of good work), but as an example of our power *over* nature and as a prelude to gluttonous, destructive consumption. When we over-consume we provide with the sense, not that we have met our family's vital needs, but that we have staved off the predators, the bill collectors, the credit agencies – those who stand between us and the real providers of the "necessities" we subscribe to.

The simple dignity of providing has been mostly lost, and with it we have lost its spirituality. Regardless, the role is still relevant, and provides one of the basic blocks of our identity and spirituality. We would do well to remember and celebrate this role. Providing is good work.

Bringer of Wealth

The *bringer of wealth* is closely related to the *provider,* but there are differences in how the two roles are perceived and therefore treated in society.

Wealth is what you have when you have more than enough, or when you *sense* that you have more than enough. Wealth is about feeling secure, and perceiving plenty. If you think of wealth in terms of creature comforts, most of us have far more in the way of wealth than did the kings of history – but that does not mean we *feel* wealthy. What we want is to feel secure *today,* with a surplus for *tomorrow.* The bringer of wealth is the one who satisfies those feelings and perceptions. For us that looks like big savings accounts, fine homes, lots of travel, good restaurants, private schools, and fancy cars.

The value of this role, for the individual and society, is ambiguous. To really grapple with this we need to look back into pre-history. For our hunting and gathering ancestors, wealth looked a lot like meat. When the hunters brought home a big animal (or more than one) the tribe knew they had more than enough. So far so good. But now, facing a surplus, the tribe needed to bring into play social mechanisms for deciding who would get how much, who would get the extra portion, or the best portion. Should it go to the elders (former hunters who regulated the hunt), or to the best hunters (those who made the wealth possible)? Surely it should not go to the women or the children. *They* were not bringers of wealth, no matter how much of the basics of life they may have provided. Wealth was a function of the hunt, which happened *away from hearth and home.* Wealth therefore belonged to those who went out and got it.

Herein lies the problem. Those who bring home wealth are given status. It is what the rest of us offer in return for getting our hands on some of the "meat." But once we start exchanging *respect* for *wealth* we begin to create destructive divisions within society.

The first division is between those who bring wealth and those who depend on it but do not directly create it. The first group is viewed positively (everyone looks up to those who bring wealth) and the second negatively (someone else did the work, and *you* should be grateful). Due to the realities of pregnancy and childcare, women have traditionally fallen into the second group.

The second division is between bringers of wealth themselves. This is the fundamental distinction between those who are "successful" and those who are not.

The consequences of these two divisions are tremendous. As we have seen, what has been traditionally thought of as "women's work" loses its value in the eyes of both men and women. Regardless of the vital role women play in the maintenance of the group, the *wealth* belongs to someone else and so, therefore, does the esteem. Women become second-class citizens. As a result, their desires, hopes, dreams, and spiritual aspirations also take second place, behind those of men.

Only in the last decades, with the growth of feminism and the increasing numbers of women entering the workforce, has this begun to change.

While the first division has not treated women kindly, the consequence of the second division (between those who are "successful" at bringing wealth and those who are not) has been no picnic for men. What happens to the man who cannot provide wealth? "Worse than a woman" is not an insult anyone is likely to mutter today, but it certainly was in the past. The hunter who could not provide wealth in days gone by, and the man who cannot provide it today, experiences this lack or inability at the core of his being. It is the source of much spiritual anguish.

In fact, there is only one "winner" in this whole scenario – the person who brings wealth. For that reason, I believe it is virtually impossible to do truly good work if this is the only role we embody. Bringing wealth is a good thing, but it must happen as a side effect of our good work.

Professional

It is hard to think of the *professional* as an archetypal role; they are a relatively new invention. But when you think of the much older role of *master*, that is, someone who has mastered a craft, then they are the logical extension of that archetype. Much like the craft masters of the past, the *professional* bears within him or herself a particular role in our community, a role which comes from both the type and manner of working.

The role of professional derives from two things: mastery of a set of skills, and recognition by a regulatory body. At one time, the regulators were guilds. Now they are professional societies or associations, or doctors' and teachers' colleges. Once you have mastered the skills deemed necessary by the regulatory body, and been accepted into their company, you are a *professional.*

This status entitles you to esteem and respect – esteem and respect by virtue of the role itself, regardless of who you are as a person. This is a curious phenomenon, and like many things about work, it is a two-edged sword. On the face of it, it is remarkable that we would value a person, not on the basis of their character, but only on the basis of mastery of skills and recognition by a professional body. Yet we do it every day.

On the other hand, the role reflects a reality: mastery needs recognition if we as a community are to live together. We need to identify those who can be trusted for their competence. We need to be able to identify whom to call upon for assistance, advice, and training. This is a profoundly important function in a complex society. We do not know each other personally. When we have a need for important services like medicine, law, or education, we cannot from the phone book white pages simply call the person who can provide the closest necessary assistance. Page after page of names rolls by and we have no idea who is the right person to contact to evaluate our illness, advise us on our mortgage, or teach our children. We have to look for those who are recognized, legitimate, and qualified, and we do so by requiring professional legitimization. That way we know that even though we personally do not know the wheres and whats of their training, the mere fact that they have the license or accreditation means that they are probably good for us.

There is yet another side effect of this role. When we become professionals, we are often changed by that recognition. Because we are trusted, we often become more trustworthy. Because we are esteemed, we often feel better about ourselves. Because we have been tested for competence we often work hard to maintain that status. As others perceive us (trusted, esteemed, competent) their perceptions become, for many of us, a standard which we try to live up to. This is not universal, and we can all identify betrayals of professional standards, but that very betrayal indicates how powerfully we expect professionals to behave in a specific way.

Despite the problems that can occur around this role, it is a profound and positive role which we need. While professional status does not ensure "good work," it gets many of us closer to that destination, and brings all of us as society into greater harmony.

Growing Person

There is another archetypal role we may embody in our work and that refers to our potential as *growing persons*. We often forget that it is in the course of our work that we meet many of the challenges through which we mature as individuals. In our work we confront people, issues, and opportunities which force us to change and grow. This has traditionally been the rationale for granting seniority and for promotion based on seniority. Ideally, at least in the past, our growth as individuals in skill, wisdom, and understanding resulted in increasing job stability, higher income, and recognition for promotion. This is not as much the case today, but even so, we still regard our transformations through work as positive contributions to our identity.

As we grow in wisdom through our work, we also grow in wisdom through all aspects of our life. Being forced to learn to deal graciously with nasty customers can set us free to deal graciously with life outside the workplace. Being challenged to learn new management methods can allow us to learn new ways to resolve other life issues.

Unfortunately, this aspect of work is often overlooked because we have tended to place work outside the bounds of what is important to our inner lives. But the sense of competence we learn, the graciousness we learn, the emotions we deal with, and the skills we pick up on the job almost always influence the rest of our lives, including our inner spiritual journey.

We will return to this at a later point because it is through this role that our work can become not just a context, but a spiritual opportunity as we journey.

Destroyer

One role which I will not spend much time on, but which must be recognized, is our role as destroyers. Our hunting and gathering ancestors left behind holes in the ground where roots grew and carcasses of what were once living animals. As we shall see in the next chapter, *all* work creates byproducts, and many of these are negative. In our work we use up resources, harm vast sections of our planet, force others to do things they would rather not do, and consume energy. This is the shadow which haunts all our work.

Transformer/Creator

The sixth role, and the one on which I want to spend the most time, is our archetypal role as *transformers* or *creators*. It is from this role that the essential nature of good work springs.

I use the term *transformer* to acknowledge the reality that *in* and *through* our work the world is transformed from one thing to another by design. Work is not random scattered activity, but is driven by human purposes or intentions. Human work is the interface between *what is* and *what could be*, and it always leads to what *will be*. Our work *creates* the future.

Our ability to transform is what gives us hope and joy. It is what creates the sense of satisfaction we feel in our work. Our ability to transform reaches *in*, to the core of our being (we are able to transform ourselves, our drives, and the images we use to define ourselves), and *out* to the farthest reaches of our space-time and culture. It is as transformers and creators that we reach the pinnacle of what it means to be human and faithful. Transformation is the essence of our spiritual journey toward good work, and it is the key to good work itself.

Our ability to transform and create is expressed in everything we do, whether we are a machinist who takes a bar of steel and turns it into a piece of equipment, or a manager who works to mold people and processes, or an environmentalist who seeks to save our natural environment, or a social activist who lobbies government for more just and equitable distribution of wealth in society. For this reason, it is a power we must consider carefully.

Until we act to transform, the future exists as a vast range of possibilities. Once we act, each one of those possibilities is either brought into being or excluded from existence by our actions. Whether I write this word or that word changes what you read, and (maybe) what you think, and (hopefully) what you do. Once I have made my choice (and my words are printed) it becomes very difficult to unmake that choice. Once I have created something, it becomes virtually impossible to uncreate it – to put the genie back into the bottle. You will read what I have written, and not something else I could have written. If we discover we have erred, we can only hope to further transform that error into something better – which demands even more work and involves further risk of misstep.

Our errors, limitations, and problems have created a world which is less than it could be. Of all possible worlds, ours is not the best, and that is our fault. It was not the best when we inherited it, and our limitations as creators ensure that it will be even less than it could have been when we die. Our actions have consequences, and they are never all positive.

It is far too easy for this ability to create to go to our heads. Just because we *can* create something does not mean we *should* create it. Forgetting that, we have let loose on the planet unimaginable potential for destruction. We have only to remember the atom bomb and other weapons of mass destruction. At a more personal level, it is not good for any one of us to get carried away with the knowledge of our power to create the future. We can become arrogant and dangerous in small ways, as well as large.

Still, this is not to deny the positive power of our place as creators. Even though the world we have inherited is less than the best, we have also been left with the possibility of redeeming the errors of those who worked before us; we can improve upon what we have been given. This type of transformation represents the very best of work.

As well, the human potential to do good is also tremendous. Even our *failures* are often magnificent, and sometimes, in a kind of cosmic ironic twist, *better* for being failures. It is as if there is a grace that gets into this world through our failures and uses them as a beginning point for something better.

Transformation is the key to good work. It is in our role as creators and transformers that we *do* good work. And so it is to the exploration of good work itself that we now turn.

3

Good Work

———————

An acquaintance, a manager in an enormous government bureaucracy, recently confided in me that he saw his work as a reflection of his beliefs and commitments, and that what he was doing was improving the world. I was a little taken aback by the confession, in part because of my long standing suspicion of bureaucrats. But as I thought about it, I realized he was correct.

While the larger bureaucracy of which he was a part was not particularly noted for its generosity, sensitivity, or compassion, I had to recall that his particular section was noted for just those characteristics. His staff were also remarkable for their high morale, and for their long-term commitment to public service, forward thinking, and flexibility. The more I thought about it, the more I became aware that he had taken his values and built a section which did its job well and nurtured its staff in the process. He had not discovered a cure for cancer, stopped pollution, ended a war, or written a transforming piece of literature, yet he had done good work.

Good Work

So what is good work? To answer that question, we must recognize that it has at least two components. First, we have the *inherent nature* of the work itself. Is there work which is good, in and of itself? I believe that there is. Second, we need to talk about our *experience* of the work we do. This is much more subjective. The question here is really, "Is this good work, *for me*?" What follows in the rest of this chapter, and in the rest of this book, is meant to answer both parts of the question, "What is good work?" To begin, let's look at the nature of good work itself.

Very simply, I use the term good work to refer to those activities which make the world a better place after they are done. Good work strives to build a more livable planet. Good work recognizes that all life – not just human life – has a right to exist, and that it requires a clean environment, the space, and the freedom to do so.

Good work – whether it involves the person at the next desk, the family who lives down the block, the community in another city, or the nation half way around the world – seeks to build healthy relationships of trust and caring and acceptance between people of all races.

Good work leaves behind it the sense that what has been done is for the better, that the little shift in the cosmic balance made by our efforts is a shift to the good. It is the type of work we are proud to proclaim as ours. It is something which excites us by its possibilities and the knowledge of what has been accomplished.

Sometimes good work results in outward visible changes. But they do not have to be huge and startling. They can be small changes, little things noticeable sometimes not even to ourselves; tiny changes which push the world in hope and expectation to something better.

Sometimes good work consists of preparing the inner ground of our lives for future growth. Good work is something which requires that we learn and grow to the depths of our being.

In doing good work, therefore, we have not only a task with regard to the world, we also have a task with regard to ourselves. Every day, we need to work in situations and environments where the potential to improve the world and ourselves is before us. It is in this sense, as I argued in the previous chapter, that good work is inherently about transformation, and that it is in our role as transformers and creators *that we do truly good work.*

Decision Making

Given what I have just said, there are going to be choices and decisions we need to make. Good work is not something which gets done by happenstance, at least not usually. We need to be able to see, as we approach points of decision, which path will lead to a better world, and which path will lead to something less desirable. Sometimes our decision making will involve very sophisticated analysis, and sometimes it will be easy to see the direction.

We will need on our journey to good work to have a picture of what a better world looks like. I have outlined in broad strokes what I consider to be the essentials of that vision. But each of us will need to be able to picture what "better" looks like in our own specific context. We will also need to learn how to measure short-term and long-term progress. Sometimes things need to get worse before they can get better, and sometimes making things better in the short-term will make things much worse in the long-term.

I believe that *everyone* is capable of doing good work. Regardless of how difficult our work situation is, how oppressive the conditions or management, we can make choices which in tiny ways make things better. It can be something as small as being polite to others, and helping each other to see the humanity we share. Even if all we do is tighten bolts on an assembly line, we are doing good work if our goal is to produce a more reliable and trustworthy product, and to build healthy relationships with our peers and supervisors. There is no place where good work cannot happen as we each make use of the options we have to move toward the best in our situation.

For most of us, our potential for good work is boundless. We face not a limited range of possibilities for good work, but an over-abundance. The question for most of us is not good versus evil, or good versus bad, but good versus better. In some respects, this is the more difficult choice. We can easily find ourselves throwing up our hands in confusion and dismay as we try to choose the "best" work.

Work

One way out of this confusion is to backtrack for a moment. We need to have a better sense of what work *is*. While we all work, very few of us have thought clearly about what it is we are doing.

I believe that all work involves seven components: imagination, intention, skills, effort, resources, products, and byproducts. Here is how it works. We start with an act of *imagination*; we envision what it is we want to do. Then we set out with the *intention* of achieving that goal. Next, using that *imaginative picture* and our *intention* to direct us, we apply our *skills* and *efforts* to some *resource*. A resource can be anything from time, to some material, to a natural resource such as a tree or some form of energy, to potential customers. As we apply our skills and efforts to this resource, it is transformed into a *product*:

perhaps a hard good like a toaster, or a service. Along the way, we always produce *byproducts*, which can be either positive or negative. On the negative side, there is always wasted energy, or unused or unusable materials. On the positive side, the byproduct of our work may be satisfied customers, or the satisfaction we feel ourselves knowing we have done our work well.

If we draw it as a diagram it looks like this:

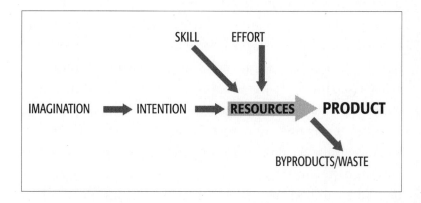

Good work, or if we are choosing between good and better, is work which reflects some sense of "good," or "better," in each of these seven areas. Good work, in its fullest sense, is work which is good at each one of these levels in both the short-term and long-term. When we find such work, where imagination, intentions, skills, efforts, resources, products, and byproducts are each good, and work together for good, we have indeed found good work, the best work.

To get a better understanding of how we can find this kind of good work, we need to see more clearly how these components interact. And to do that we need to look at each individually.

IMAGINATION

To transform the world, or anything else, requires first of all an act of imagination. We must be able to imagine a possible outcome before we can proceed. We must be able to hold in our heads some sort of imagined consequence of our actions before we can guide our body to perform the necessary work. We must be able to imagine how the resources at our command can be manipulated into the shape and form we need to accomplish our desires.

For an architect, this involves the ability to hold a whole building in his or her head, to imagine people living and working within a massive physical structure. Then this imagining must be re-imagined as models and lines on paper which can be used to guide other people's imaginations. Engineers must take what has been put on paper and be able to imagine what sort of materials, steel locations, reinforcements, conduits, and wiring will be necessary to make the building come alive. Still other workers must be able to imagine how these lines and directions are to take shape as actual forms for concrete, ducting for heat, and wiring for electricity. Imagination brings a building into being, an imagination that operates for each person involved in this work from inception to final touch of paint.

We use our imaginations so often and so naturally, that we tend to lose sight of the magic of what we are doing. Furthermore, it is difficult to describe the connection between good work and imagination in a way that is not circular, because whatever we decide constitutes good work is itself the product of our imagination. At the beginning of the chapter I said that good work strives to build a more livable planet and to nurture positive human relationships. I then tried to describe, if only in very broad strokes, what each of those things entailed. In doing so, I was imagining or envisioning what I consider to be a better world. And while I would argue that those things are not just good from my particular, subjective point of view, but are good in some absolute objective sense, they are still the product of an imaginative process.

The best I can do at this point is to say that we need to think carefully about the values we bring to our imaginative process (more about this in the next chapter) and about what the consequences would be for other people and the world should what we imagine become reality.

INTENTIONS

We face much the same problem when trying to define good intentions, and their relationship to imagination, but we can at least say this: it must be with good intentions that we bring what we have imagined to reality. Somewhere, behind all good work, is someone who intends something good to happen. Ideally, a hairstylist has as his intention good looking customers. If he does not, then something other than "good" work has been done.

The thing about our intentions is that they are never entirely clear or pure. As a hairstylist, I may want to produce good looking customers, but I also have an idea in my own mind of what a good looking customer looks like, an idea which may not be shared by my customer. As the customer service revolution has tried to point out, a good intention, at least in part, is one which the *customer* perceives as good, and that is not always the same as what I, the worker, intend.

But it is not adequate simply to gauge our intentions against those of our customers. Customers can be wrong, and often are. When it comes to discerning the depth and breadth of human intentions, it is not hard to conclude that *all* intentions are bad, not only the customer's, but also our own. We do not know enough to have genuinely good intentions. We are all too immersed in our own issues and confusions to ever "intend" perfectly. Our lives are too fogged by partial perceptions, by hopes and dreams, by pains and fears.

To make matters even more complex, few of us work solely on the basis of our own intentions. Those of us who work for other people are particularly dependent upon the intentions of others. And they in turn are dependent upon other people's intentions. The web of intentions stretches out in long and confusing strands.

However, we need not follow this confusing web to the point of certainty. The most important thing, for those of us doing the work, is our own intentions. We can insist that, as far as possible, the intention behind our work is the creation of a better world. We can look at ourselves in the mirror and be clear that, through our work, we want to see the world become a cleaner, healthier place, where good relationships flourish and people are pushed to grow.

The key point is to question our intentions in the first place. If all we are after is money or an easy time we will know it. And if we are trying to build a better world through what we do, we will know that too. Never with absolute certainty, which means that we can never stop asking the question, but with enough clarity that we can either continue what we are doing, or know that either our intentions or our work needs to change.

The other aspect of intentions is planning. Good intentions are mapped, organized to accomplish goals. We need to be clear *what* we intend to do, and *when* and *how* we intend to do it, in order to accomplish good work. Without a plan, our good intentions get squandered in frustrated aimlessness. It is not that we do not know what we want to accomplish, but that we do not know what route to take. Planning, of course, can be a form of work all its own. Planning is a major supervisory task. Yet it is also something each of us needs to do. We *all* need to have a plan, even if the only goal we have is to be a nicer person.

SKILL

A skill is something we use to make our intentions a reality. Without skills, intentions remain just that – good intentions. We use skills to turn the resources with which we work into products. We may have the highly sophisticated skills of a software engineer, or the simple skills of a parking lot attendant.

Skills are something we possess to either a greater or lesser degree. I once had the opportunity to work with a group of highly skilled individuals on a very complex project which had to be completed within a very short time frame. It was a wonderful experience. We did good work, and we got it done with tremendous satisfaction along the way. I have also had the opportunity to work with task groups which were not adequately skilled. We still got the work done, but it was not as pleasurable, nor was the outcome as good. It was not bad work, but it was a long way from what a better trained group could have accomplished. Good work requires good skills.

An obvious corollary is that those who wish to do good work need to pursue excellence in their skills. Once our intentions are as good as we can make them, then we need to ensure that our skills are up to the task. In our changing world, this means constant improvement. There is no such thing as mastery in any field without the willingness to keep learning. The target keeps shifting, and good work requires that we keep up.

It may be worth adding that good tools go hand in hand with good skills. Without tools, skills cannot be used. With *good* tools, good skills become excellence applied. The better the tools, the better the work.

EFFORT

The fourth thing we bring to our work is effort. It takes energy, drive, and commitment to do good work. Those who do not bring these things will fall short, produce substandard or less than excellent products. Good work requires that we put ourselves into our tasks with enthusiasm, looking for every opportunity to achieve or improve upon our best.

RESOURCES

Resources are the things which we convert, under the direction of intentions, through the application of skills and effort. The hairstylist's resources are the customer's hair, the dyes, shampoos, electricity, and water he uses. The urban planner's resources are the focus groups, the engineering studies, the demographic projections, and the council meetings. She converts these into good plans for the city. No matter what sort of work we do, there are resources, inputs, which we convert into outputs or products.

The quality of resources available to us can vary widely. The best work requires good resources.

However, here there is a special category of good work. It involves making "more" out of "less." This type of good work is especially worth recognizing in a world of dwindling resources, where resources need to be shared more equitably. Making more out of less means there is more to go around. It usually also leads to fewer negative byproducts such as waste or pollution. When we are able to do this, we are truly doing good work.

PRODUCTS

Good products are the most complex part of the work process. What makes them complex is that not only is their goodness a reflection of the intentions, skill, effort, and resources that went into them, a complex enough equation to begin with, but once they have been produced they take on a life of their own. Once a product is available, it can be used by others to do things which may not reflect any of the goodness which went into its production. Or it can be used to do things much better than any use the worker could have imagined. The pick-up truck used to transport food to famine stricken areas is doing a good work and fulfilling a goodness of which its assemblers may have had no conception. The razor sharp cooking knife used to threaten a co-worker is a danger and not the excellent tool its manufacturer intended.

This complexity cannot be *managed*. A product, once it is produced, is literally outside our control. We cannot know if our products will be used well or poorly, within the range intended, or in some other way unimagined. However, our responsibility does not end once the product is produced. When bad uses of our product take place we must go back and ask ourselves, "Could we have made this product in such a way that this bad use was impossible, or less likely?" This question must be directed at each step of the way: Could we have imagined better? Could we have intended better? Could we have been more skillful? Could we have applied better effort? Could we have used better resources, or used our existing resources better? Ideally, a bad use of our product becomes the opportunity to improve our product. Bad uses can be a critical spur to "better" work.

We also need to take into account the decay process as the product or service reaches the end of its life. An excellent haircut is one which continues to stay neat even as the hair becomes longer and shaggier. A PCB filled electrical transformer reveals its nature as a bad work only when it reaches the end of its life and becomes a health hazard. How a product leaves the cycle of existence tells us as much about the goodness of the work as anything else. A city plan which continues to enlighten and promote a healthy vision of the city, even as its projections become out of date, is an excellent one and demonstrates the full goodness of the work which went into it.

Ideally, good products become "classic" products. Classic products are those we look back upon as milestones, special markers of the excellence of our work. These become both points of tremendous satisfaction (especially when others recognize the value of that special product) and the standards of excellence for our and others' future work. Classics are not just better, they stand for the *best* that could be done and point the way for other *excellent* products.

BYPRODUCTS

Byproducts are the intended and unintended, positive or negative secondary outcomes produced through our work. A paycheque is a *positive* byproduct which most of us receive due to our work. Other positive byproducts include the satisfaction and esteem our good work may generate. At the same time, our work always produces *negative* byproducts. This is one of the fundamental laws of the universe. Waste, for example, is a negative byproduct of all work. Good work should minimize the negative by products and maximize the good ones.

Room for Improvement

Imagination, intentions, skills, effort, resources, products, and byproducts: these are the pieces of work, and we all use them. Whether we start with the dream of a clean house and end with the byproduct of family happiness, or we begin with the goal of company profitability and end with increased stock prices, all the work we do incorporates these seven pieces. When all these pieces are good (or as good as we are capable of making them) then we are doing good work.

Defining good work in this way puts a tremendous responsibility on our shoulders. Whether good work happens is in large measure up to us. Ideally, as we examine each of these seven parts of our work, we find that we are proud of the good work we are doing. I suspect, however, that as we struggle to do good work there will always be things we can improve. We can allow ourselves more "free" space and time to imagine creatively. We can be clearer about our intentions. We can develop our skills. We can apply more consistent effort. We can select better resources. We can refine the product, or change some of the byproducts. There is almost always something we can do better. This, too, is part of good work and we can take pride in our drive to improve.

There is even a positive byproduct of our good work which I have not yet mentioned. Usually our work does not go unnoticed. Once we start doing good work, those around us find that the standards for *their* work have changed. Each small change we make – to produce more, or to improve our skills – sets in front of others a new possibility, one that they will either move toward or react against. Usually people are drawn to do better. Most of us *want* to do good work, and when faced with a better alternative we work to adopt it.

A few, however, will see our attempt to do good work as a criticism or a violation, and struggle to make things worse. Many a young worker, full of zeal to do good work, has faced the displeasure of older workers used to other ways, or a less productive pace. Regardless, good workers focus on *remaining* good workers, taking whatever comes their way as a resource in their struggle to make themselves better. By doing so, they help others move further along their own path to good work.

Good work is the *end* and the *means*. It is the *goal* toward which we strive and the *method* by which we achieve it. We all want to find the point where we can say with satisfaction, "Well done." But even to strive to find that continually shifting point is to do good work. Every step, every effort, puts in front of us and others a new target, a new hope, a new possibility.

The Experience of Work

While we now have a sense of what good work is in its external mode, there is a second dimension to work, and that is our *experience* of it. However, here it is not so easy to say, "this is good work" or "that is good work." We need to say, instead, "that is good work for her" and "this is good work for me." Each of us experiences work differently based on our abilities, personality, experience, needs, state of development, and goals. Work that I find immensely satisfying, my "good work," may be work that drives you to frustration, and the reverse may also be true. We are each different and experience work differently.

While none of us can define someone else's good work, we can map this experience. Even though what is good for me may not be good for you, when *my* work is *not* good for me, I experience much the same things as you experience when *your* work is *not* good for you. Likewise, when you and I feel good about our work, even though we may be doing very different things, we both feel good in much the same way, for very similar reasons.

Labor

Sometimes, we experience work as labor. And labor is something positive. Think of how we use the term in speech. We often speak of a "labor of love." We also refer to a woman's effort in childbirth as labor. This latter example illustrates especially well the unique character of labor.

Labor refers to the effort we expend and the opportunity we have to express ourselves and our convictions through our work. It is the part of work which is shaped by, and in some measure reflects, our identity. Each of us, no matter how routine or standardized our work, leaves a mark, a trace of our passing on our work. Labor is also our experience of living through our work. When we labor, we find ourselves giving life to something important to us. When we end our labor it is with satisfaction.

This is most obvious for those who work in jobs where the human component is central. Creativity, relational sensitivity, and insight are important parts of many jobs and these things emerge from who we are and what we believe about the world. The doctor's "bedside manner" is a key part of how she heals. The sales person puts himself into the relationship with the customer. The work of the artist or architect, strategic planner or writer all show the signs of their creator's vision, personality, beliefs, and energy. Those with the opportunity to do these kinds of work sometimes find in their labor something almost transcendent, an experience of creator and cosmos moving into harmony.

But labor is also present in more technical jobs. The mechanic demonstrates a way of working with parts or the house painter uses a quality of paint and craftsmanship which reflect his understanding of quality. The mechanic who works on my car is someone special. His love of motors and his concern for cars is something which he exudes as he works. I know that when he is done my car has been worked on, not only by someone with technical ability, but also by someone with a deep commitment to the well-being of my car. He drags me from one car to the next in the shop, showing me the various components, explaining the costs of various parts, and how he works to ensure cars work well at the lowest cost to their owners. Competent car repair I can get many places, but this level of commitment is something for which I willingly pay extra. For my mechanic, car repair is an experience of labor.

Even in rote manufacturing, labor is involved. In simple assembly line nuts and bolts work, there is labor. An angry person will cross thread more, have a generally lower level of productivity, and be harder to work with than will someone who puts their will and happiness into the job. We always have the opportunity to express a little of who we are and what we believe in our work.

Knowing that we labor can be liberating. Once we know that we always have an impact through the work we do, we can strive to maximize that impact. When I know that my smile changes the situation I can improve my work by smiling more frequently. If I know that a little extra care in my work can be an expression of my belief in caring for the world, I will feel better about my work and, in many cases, others will feel better about me too. When we are able to release our inner beings into the labor of our work, we have the potential to become one with our work.

I believe that the possibility of labor is an expression of the presence of love in the universe. It means that no matter where we are, no matter what our circumstances, we can make a genuine impact for the better. Through our labor, we give birth to a profoundly better world and we, in turn, are humanized and enabled to grow.

Toil

There is another side to the experience of work. Regardless of who we are, how sainted we might be, or what we do, part of our work hurts us. That destruction may be of ourselves – physically, mentally, or spiritually – or destructive of those around us, or of the planet itself. There is a part of what we do that makes us and the world worse. This is the tragedy of work. This is toil.

We all experience part of our work as a "grind," as difficult, as a struggle, or as something hurtful. It can be as little as having to show up for work on a regular basis; for some of us, routine is very hard to take. For others it may be that their workplace is an abusive, soul destroying combination of anger, poor working conditions, waste, and danger.

One of the terrible ironies for those in the helping professions, particularly for psychotherapists, is that they must sometimes assist in destruction in order to build. To help one person with a damaged inner being to recover, they must sometimes walk alongside as their client destroys relationships, hurts those close to them, and suffers great agonies. A journey of healing can leave great damage in its wake, a damage which the therapist feels, and sometimes finds personally destructive.

The negative consequences of toil can be extreme. Some bosses work their staffs to destruction, bullying and preying on psychological weakness until staff are ready to break. Some jobs simply demand so much of people, that they are unable to contribute to their families, friends, or communities. Some jobs prey on customers, exploiting their weaknesses for money. Some jobs leave immense ecological destruction in their wake. The toil here infects whole communities.

Sometimes the toil is due to who we are in our work. While I was a graduate student, I spent four years working part-time as a clerk in a library. The job paid well and gave me time to work on my thesis and attend classes. It was an excellent situation for any student. But it also ground me down. There was no activity which was not written down in the operations manual or scheduled down to the minute. The routine was immense and stultifying. I experienced the lack of opportunity to contribute or change things as a prison. After four years the stress was almost intolerable and I suffered obvious physical side effects and some not so obvious ones.

But I have to admit that my personality was the major factor here, not something inherent in the job. I worked in a department of four, and at least two of the other three staff enjoyed their work immensely. These two showed an enthusiasm for the routine which amazed me.

They obviously enjoyed what they did and where they did it. Clearly, what made that job toil for me was a combination of my personality and my expectations. I am an imaginative, creative person. I love change. I treasure the opportunity to contribute new ideas and methods. Closely managed routine work is something which I will always experience as toil.

In contrast, I have noticed that the working conditions under which I thrive – high stress, deadline ridden, development filled, and cutting edge – are conditions that many people find very difficult. What sends me humming to sleep is enough to drive some up the walls. They find to be toil what I would not trade for anything.

This can be taken as an excuse for wishing we were other than we are, for trying to match our personalities to our work. I believe it is easier and better to change the type of work we do so that it matches the type of people we are. Our work should not leave us angry at the end of each day. It should not bring us down. It should not be overwhelming emotional toil. Our work should not destroy us.

Even the best work will have some element of toil, just as the worst work has some element of labor. Good work usually has less toil than labor. But both labor and toil are present in differing degrees, degrees known only to each of us. They are the *experience* of work.

Vocation

One final way of thinking about work which we need to examine before we can go on is that of vocation. For centuries people have had "vocations," work which was both a *calling* and understood to be permanent, a lifetime commitment. Now we face a world where the idea of *belonging to your work* seems ridiculous. At the same time, very little is permanent any longer and very few types of work will last as long as we will. It seems that the concept of vocation is obsolete.

Yet we cannot put the concept aside. I recently had a conversation with a woman who has found her calling. She knows and feels with the fullness of her being that her place is with her children and so she has elected to stay home with them. She did this despite ability, education, and a social location which suggested that she had other good options. She may have had doubts, but my impression is that she is serene in her decision. Her vocation is that of "mother and homemaker." For her, vocation is still a very relevant concept, and while the "vocation" itself may not be permanent, it is at least long-term.

I know of other people who strive to find their vocation. They search for the work of their hearts, the place where they can apply their energy with the knowledge that of the many possibilities in the universe, this is the one *to which they belong*. Some find it, and others do not.

But even for those who are *not* looking for a "vocation" in this sense, there is something valuable in this concept. But before I look at that, I want to express two cautions.

To understand vocation as "permanent occupation" is probably a bad idea, and those who think of it and pursue it in this fashion are headed, I believe, for disappointment. As attractive as the idea of having a *single* "soul" vocation may be, life itself seems to find its way through an openness to change. To live in harmony with life, we must be able to satisfy our desire for "soul work," or meaning, within sometimes chaotic circumstances.

This caution is based on personal experience. At one time, I held this view I am cautioning against. In the midst of life's happenstance and mystery, I kept looking for a way out, a way to find quiet and good order, and I thought that if I found my "true" work I would find that peace. Now, as I look back, I realize that I found the most resonance between myself and my work when I learned to ask the question, "What am I *called* to do *in this situation*?"

I believe that life is a shifting collection of experiences and opportunities, a web of unceasing possibility, where we move along lines partly of our own volition, and partly at the hands of those around us. To live well and effectively in the midst of this, we need to be able to maintain balance, seeing both the good possibilities and the bad possibilities around us. As long as we stress *a specific, singular* vocation we are blind to both. As long as we think we know where we are going, we are unable to stare clear-eyed at the possibilities before us; we keep looking for those which fit our sense of "vocation" but ignore even the best of possibilities which do not.

I have one more caution. Sometimes our own destructive desires are misinterpreted as a vocation. This is a terrible problem for us in North America, as given as we are to making decisions based on our feelings. One of my staff once confessed to me his own sense of vocation. It troubled me because it seemed to cover up serious personal issues. I perceived his "sense" of vocation as being a way of hiding from who he was, not as a foundation for a life of good work.

But this concept has, as I said, certain strengths. Vocation is a powerful way of expressing and feeling our belief that we have unique abilities as individuals to do specific kinds of good work. It is something most of us experience from time to time, though rarely continuously.

There are times in the midst of our day-to-day workplace activity when we find ourselves *resonating* with our job, and we "know" that in that particular space and time the work "belongs" to us. Something about the way we did the work, the skills we applied, the specific energy or imagination we brought, or the intention or resources we used spoke of our character, beliefs, and values in such a way that we felt a strong sense of ownership. Usually, those are moments of satisfaction because not only was that specific piece of work ours, it was also well done. We know, about a specific accomplishment, that it was *our* work and it was *good* work. It is our *calling* to do this work, and when we actually *respond* to that call and *do* it, we experience our *vocation*.

This experience of vocation may be occasional or it may be sustained. When it is sustained we know we are doing not only *good work*, but *better* work, perhaps even the *best* work. It is to finding and maintaining this experience that we turn next.

4

Career Direction for the Soul

—▬—

Finding our vocation is no easy task. When I was in high school, I had the inevitable chat with the guidance counselor about my future. I sat there, 16, gangly and naive, and told him I was interested in architecture.

"Why do you want to do that?" he asked me in a tone I interpreted as negative. He continued, "Have you done any research? Do you know what's involved?" Good questions, sort of. Unfortunately, I had no answers. I did not know what architects actually did, let alone what research would be appropriate. So I sat there. I cannot remember how our interview ended, but I am sure the counselor thought he was wasting his time. For my part, I left his office with the conclusion that architecture was a bad idea. I did not know what I wanted, and beyond some vague idea that designing buildings would be a good thing, I had no idea what I should do.

Years later, I discovered that architecture would have been a good option to pursue. I have a lot of design ability, a good head for math and engineering, and a love of human structures. I am also highly creative. Whether I would actually have *made* a good architect is another question, and one that will remain unanswered.

What the situation with the counselor illustrates is both the enormity of the questions confronting anyone facing a career shift (whether at mid-life or when just starting out), and the difficulty in knowing how to approach these questions as searchers.

Most of us, I believe, want more than just a job. We seek belonging, consistency, stability, and satisfaction, all the things which come with doing what we are *supposed* to do. We want the comfort of being able to put our ability and energy into some aspect of human life which will allow us to say, "It is good." We want work which *resonates* with our souls, *our* good work. The problem is in identifying that work. One of my teachers once said, "There are two tasks in life. The first is to find out what you want to do. The second is to find someone to pay you to do it." It is my belief that the former task is harder than the latter.

As I said in the last chapter, life is chaotic. And as the first chapter pointed out, jobs can be very transient. Then there are the problems related to finding an appropriate job in the first place. There are approximately 20,000 occupations which one might pursue. Within each of these, there are many subcategories. Nor is the situation getting simpler. Every year more new occupations appear than old ones disappear. It is no easy task to sort through these thousands to determine which is the right one for us. It means learning about the requirements you need to begin, the range of tasks involved, the opportunities available, the type of supervision in place, the supports and working conditions to be found – all the many things which make a job more or less desirable to us or possible for us. Faced with this situation, it is an unfortunate reality that, left to our own, we are unlikely ever to be able to say with certainty that "This is *my* task." Often, the best we can say is, "I enjoy what I am doing!"

This last is no small thing, and for some people it is enough. One of life's great gifts is to be given work you enjoy most of the time. If you have stumbled to that place you may count yourself blessed. Far too many of us never even get to that point. We end up stuck in tolerable work, but not *enjoyable* work, or even in intolerable work to which we can see no alternative. To enjoy the work we have is a wonderful gift.

Regardless, I believe we each have within us the drive to find our special place in the universe, that place where we know we are doing what we should be doing. We search for that place where there is a harmony between our soul and our actions, and where we experience the pieces of our lives coming together as they should. We need to find the place where we experience our vocation – our good work – on a regular basis.

Career Planning Basics

Abilities

When I think about what happened those many years ago in the guidance counselor's office, I realize my real problem at the time was not even the one I thought I had. I wanted more than anything to know what I *should* be doing, to find my good work, my vocation, and I wanted that counselor to help me. Unfortunately, as is so often the case with spiritual tasks, I was not asking the right question. I needed to ask an even more basic question. What I needed to know at that point was what I *could* do.

What we *should* do, our good work, is something contained within the range of what we *can now do*, or *could do* with more training and experience. While I have found people who were determined to do what was obviously impossible for them to do (more on them later), I am convinced that *we are never genuinely called to do that which we cannot do.* The place to start, then, is with our abilities, with what we can do.

The list of things we can do includes that enormous range of abilities, training, and experiences we possess. It is not, as often thought, made up of a collection of past job descriptions. Each of us has a huge range of things we can actually or potentially do, and only a few of them may ever have been part of our job description.

Let's look at abilities. Each of us has certain innate and biological capabilities. These both limit us and open up possibilities to us. I am severely shortsighted and slightly asthmatic. These limit some of the things I can do. I am highly creative. This expands what I can do. I have also learned how to do many things: write well, talk to groups, plan processes, research, organize groups, and so on. Altogether, this collection of physical and psychological characteristics, combined with skills I have learned, represents my abilities. Each of us has a unique range and selection of abilities. I may be able to do what you cannot, and vice versa. For most of us, our abilities are numbered in the thousands.

In part, we identify our abilities from the names other people give them and the contexts we are used to using them in. I may think of my abilities as those of a junior soccer coach, for example, when it might be more accurate to say I have the ability to motivate, instruct, organize, and strategize, particularly with children. All too often, however, our abilities are a mystery to us. We never have an opportunity to explore many of our capabilities in order to turn them into abilities, and we may even be only partially aware of the abilities we have developed. This is one of the reasons nearly every job or career transition book has a section on naming abilities, which usually includes a list of hundreds of potential abilities.

Then, of course, we must assess the relative *strength* of our abilities. While many of us have the ability to write, and nearly all of us have the ability to speak, few of us know how to write well and some of us are not able to speak well. The same is true for most other abilities. While we may be *able*, we may not be particularly *well able*, and this means that even when abilities go by the same name, they are not really the same. While it is important for a parent to be able to diagnose and respond to the difference between a low and a high fever, this does not mean that they can realistically list medical diagnosis as an ability. We would expect a much higher level of competence from one who claimed that ability. So when listing our abilities it is important to be honest in rating how they compare to the abilities of others. We need also to recognize that each of us has the potential to develop more abilities or greater skill in the ones we already possess. What we can do now need not be the same as what we can do six months or a year from now.

One of the hardest parts of a career counselor's life is dealing with people who have no clue about the importance of ability. These are the people who strongly believe that they should be doing something that it is obvious they cannot do. They are also an employer's nightmare. I have counseled such people and on occasion I have hired such people. They have their eyes set on a destination they cannot achieve and are all too often convinced that this inability is your fault. For most of us, finding our good work is a long and sometimes painful task, and being honest about our limits is one of the vital steps we must take.

Interests

Our *interests* are another good indicator of where to look for our good work. What is it that we find ourselves doing when we have time, energy, and resources to ourselves? Do we sit in a rocking chair and gaze at the sunset? Or do we join a sporting team? Do we draw up plans for home renovations, or work in the garden? What do we do when we are free to choose? If we follow our interests, we know that regardless of where we go, we are aimed in roughly the right direction.

If, as I believe, we need the parts of our lives to fit together, then we are constantly scanning the world around us with an unconscious radar. Whenever we find something close to our soul, our inner radar goes "ah ha!" and tells us to get a little closer. This does not mean that the path to our good work will be a straight line. Often our paths meander as we confront the demands of our inner lives and as we react to the events life throws our way. Our interests now may not be our interests by the time we find our good work; they may not even be *good* interests, but I am certain they are crucial to our journey.

If that counselor had asked me what I was interested in back in high school, I might have answered two things: reading and building model cars, neither of which was terribly unusual for a boy of 16 who had not yet discovered girls. If he had pushed further, he would have found that my favorite reading was Science Fiction, and of Science Fiction my favorite was the technical kind built on scientific and technical fact. If he had had an opportunity to examine my model cars he would have discovered that I did a lot of research into what tiny bits and details went where. I had even taken automotives at school in order to improve my knowledge. In short, the counselor would immediately have seen that technical things interested me.

Logical career suggestions he could then have made may have included something in the sciences, or technical or engineering careers – even architecture! (These would also have been in keeping with my courses in high school; I took as many sciences as possible and got kicked out of English.) He could have explained the various types of jobs and employment these fields offered and asked me if any seemed to appeal to me. This approach would have built upon my interests and encouraged me to move toward an area which clearly attracted me.

Searching out interests and following these is not just a method for high school students. In fact, it works better for adults changing careers. As adults, we know a lot more about what we enjoy doing. Life throws a variety of experiences at us and we end up discovering interests we did not know we possessed. Scanning a university calendar one day I discovered a subject called sociology. It intrigued me and I took a course. I took another, and another. Then I looked for similar courses: anthropology, psychology, then geography and history. I dropped computer science. Stopped taking math. New experiences showed me that I was "really" interested in subjects and possibilities far different from where I started. I never did finish an engineering program; instead I graduated with a major in sociology and a minor in psychology.

Ten years later I changed careers again. I began by looking at what I had found most interesting in my previous job, the administrative tasks. Deciding to build on that, I went looking for a social services administrative position. I found one as the manager of a social services department with a relief and development organization.

Along the way, I discovered that I loved writing, and started free-lancing the occasional article. Public speaking attracted me too, so I started putting together presentations on various topics and then, once I saw the need, a whole series on social services management. From interest to interest to interest, I have made my way.

This method, as I have said, does not produce a simple, linear career track. Regardless, guiding our career by our interest is the right way to go. Our interests are very powerful reflections of the basic patterns of our lives. They reflect our emotional, psychological, and physical make up. Once we set them free, they will steer us a course through the huge range of things we can do and the huge range of things there are available to do. Once we are on track with our interests, our work becomes interesting, motivating, and satisfying. Interests are not a direct route to our good work, but they usually draw us close, and they keep us motivated for the journey.

Values

The next question to ask ourselves is, "What do we value?" For most of us, we can only answer this question on the basis of experience.

One of my greatest personal satisfactions has been to engage myself wholeheartedly in my work because I know that the outcome meets my deepest hopes. When I give a seminar, I know that the information I pass on is information I believe people genuinely need. With my presentation skills I have been offered "speaking packages," an arrangement whereby I become nothing more than a "mouthpiece" with no real influence on the content. I have turned these offers down. While it is nice to know that public speaking skills are in demand, I find far more pleasure in presenting my own material. I find that pleasure because I know that every word I say resonates with what I believe is truly important for people. The same is true for those I meet who do work they believe in. They have more energy, more joy, and more love for the work they are doing when they see that it reflects their deepest values.

We must become wise to our values and see them as keys to good work. Channeling our career along the lines of our values will bring us more satisfaction than any of the other career "markers," such as wealth or status or power. In fact, we will become more like "saints" in our work – selfless, hard working, compassionate, dedicated, and contributing. When we are wise to our values, and work with them, we begin to build the type of world we want to live in.

This is not the place to launch into an extended dialogue on the values we have, or should have. My concern is more with how our values affect our career directions.

First, however, I need to point out that not all values are the same. There are values which I call "deep values" and which I will deal with next. There are also other values which I call "preferences." It is *preferences* which form the basis for what little discussion of values can be found in most career direction handbooks. The difference between these two is that deep values tend to be imbedded in our psycho-social-biological make-up. They are the result of early experiences and the outcome of our developmental process. Deep values are something which we carry as part of who we are and change only rarely and with difficulty. Preferences, on the other hand, while they may be powerful, can change or be overruled without a great deal of difficulty. While it is helpful to know about them, they do not make or break the pursuit of our good work.

MAINTENANCE

I believe that all of us share at least three deep values which influence our career choices. First, we value our lives immensely and are willing to work extremely hard to *maintain* our physical, social, psychological, and spiritual well-being. This is one of the key reasons we work, for if we did not value our lives we would give up whenever we met sustained adversity. Through much of human history this value has been seen as the *only* reason for work, and has also been one of the main reasons work gets described as drudgery or toil. We are willing to do a lot to sustain our lives, including things we hate.

This points out the *negative* influence this value can have on our journey to our good work. It can lead us to accept work which runs against what is otherwise important to us, when there may be other options. While we must recognize and honor this value, we should not let it determine our lives. That way lies stagnation, frustration, and spiritual emptiness. Our work will mean more to us than just maintenance if it is truly our good work.

The *positive* influence of this value upon us is our drive for self-preservation. Wisdom with this value means knowing how far and how much we can risk before we succumb to anxiety, or worse. It is useful to have a high tolerance for risk if you are a tree-faller, or parachute jumping instructor, or venture capitalist. Others, like myself, are willing to take risks, but in moderation. We are happy to do work which may take us around the globe, or risk our prestige with colleagues, or sacrifice part of our savings to start a new business. Still others have little tolerance for risk. For them the pursuit of job stability is their number one desire. Our good work usually helps us maintain our lives and falls within the range of our risk tolerance.

PRODUCTIVE MEMBERSHIP

The second deep value we share is the opportunity to contribute to our collective well-being. While this seems to run counter to the spirit of our age, with its drive for self-actualization and its worship of the solitary hero, the reality is otherwise for most of us. Most of us want to contribute positively to our circle of friends, co-workers, and acquaintances. Most of us want to be productive members of a community which works together.

This is partly why many of us stay with the work we are doing. We have a community where our contributions are recognized. When we have the opportunity to be part of such a community of work, it is as if a tremendous weight has been lifted. We take more pride in our work, and seek the opportunity to be a good member.

Like most things to do with the soul, this desire is not always a blessing. This value can lead us into dark circumstances when the group we enjoy being part of has goals which are destructive. It is hard to break free of a work group engaged in destructive activities, when the group is accepting and encouraging of our efforts. I remember my own struggle when faced with a co-worker who was very friendly and supportive of my work in difficult circumstances, who then wanted me to help him send a highly destructive memo to senior management. I refused and the scene in my office when I did so was not pretty. I still regret the loss of relationship with him. And what, I wonder, would someone have done who needed his approval more than I did?

These negative examples simply indicate how deeply we value this sense of productive cooperation, and how wisely we must respond to it. Rare is the person who can enter a work group saying, "I do not care what they think." Most of us bend very quickly, and woe to us if we do not understand this value and work with it carefully.

As an employer, this value plays a big part in whom I hire. To me, it is more important to find someone who can work with me and the other members of the work team, than to find someone with superb skills. There is a tricky balance to be kept here, because I do not want work teams which dissolve into mushy embraces at every opportunity, or teams which spend all their time supporting one another. But I also do not want work teams where the members spend more time scrapping than working. I have seen both, and neither is good. I need people who work together respectfully and appreciatively. We need *community* at work, but it must not take the place of work itself.

REPRODUCTION

A third deep value we share is that of reproduction. By this I do not mean biological reproduction, though for many of us it includes that, but the deep satisfaction we gain when the world looks back at us with our own eyes. Most of us have an intense desire for a world which reflects to us that which we are. For many of us, this value drives us to reshape the world in our own image, or to find a place in the world which will reinforce our image.

Though most of us enjoy stepping out of our world from time to time (isn't that what tourism is all about?) what we really value is *home*, and home is not as much a physical place, or a set of relationships, as it is an emotional space. Our efforts at reproduction, then, are efforts at creating an atmosphere which is comforting to us (and not necessarily to anyone else) and secure. We seek and rearrange, sometimes desperately, the relationships and items in the world around us in order to create circumstances which reproduce the image of "home" which lies inside our heads.

Personally, I enjoy chaos quite a lot. For me, chaos speaks of opportunity, and opportunity is part of "home." Whenever I can, I build a working environment which is quite chaotic. Roles are never straightforward, tasks are always ambiguous, and it is difficult to say when things are done. As a boss, these are the things I enjoy seeing, they reflect what is inside my head, and I gain tremendous satisfaction from seeing them come to life in the world around me. On the other hand, I have told the story of working in a stringently ordered environment. While my colleagues seemed to motor along quite well, I found the policy book destructively confining. I finally quit, with great relief, and quite a few stress symptoms. Not only could I not remake the work in my image, its structure ran deeply contrary to my image of what I want the world to be like.

Again, this value tends to be disregarded in most of the career material. We rarely recognize in our guidance practices how deeply this value affects us. This may be because those of us of Western European extraction (at whom most career guidance material is aimed) share a profoundly similar sense of how the world looks. Our workplace reproductive urges tend, just like our children, to reflect our white skin. However, this overlooks the diversity we genuinely experience, and which our increasingly multicultural world is forcing onto us. It is far easier to find culturally intolerable working arrangements now than it was not many years ago. We need, in ways almost beyond imagining, to see the world in our own image, and wisdom requires that we take this into account.

OTHER DEEP VALUES

Besides these three deep values which I believe we all share, there are also those deep values that are unique to each one of us and discovered either in flashes of insight or through long living. These values are the result of the accumulated experiences of our lives and the shape of our souls and they are never the same from one person to the next. One of my own, particular deep values is my desire that the world make sense. I know other people for whom child safety, for example, represents a deep value.

Regardless of what our deep values are, it is essential that we discover them. If we do not, they will discover us, usually in painful ways. We violate our deep values only at great cost, and we rarely do so except when we find a conflict between them (such as when the value we place on productive membership clashes with our value of reproduction). Wisdom requires that we treat these values as givens and seek work and life options which allow us to engage them fully and in life-giving ways. Our failure to do so will haunt us.

It is not always an easy task to discover or map our deep values. While I valued a sensible universe long before I sat in that high school guidance counselor's office, more than ten years would pass before I began to gain a sense of it, and nearly 20 years would pass before I could put words to it. The good news is that at least three deep values are relatively common and we only need to pay attention to how they have expressed themselves in our lives. Those values which may be particular to us may take longer to understand, but by following our interests, by doing what feels good, we will come close. (This does not mean we should always seek to "feel good," but it *does* mean our deep sense of satisfaction says something very important to us about ourselves.) How we respond to suffering or to strong obstacles in our lives will also point the way to our deep values.

PREFERENCES

Then there are our preferences. These values occasionally show up in career search materials. They are most commonly presented as a paired list: do you value this or that? Do you value creativity or do you value established routine? Do you prefer to work alone or do you prefer to work with others? While these preferences are interesting, and sometimes helpful when evaluating a specific type of work, most of them will bend or change considerably in light of our deep values and I do not believe we need to worry too much about them. Once we know and are working with our deep values, these secondary values or preferences will arrange themselves to fit.

One of the best examples of this phenomenon is the value we place on money. Many career direction books ask us to rate (among other things) how important money is to us and then on that basis to evaluate particular career options. For example, pursuing a career in child care is not a good idea if making lots of money is something you value highly; childcare workers are generally among the most poorly paid workers. But my experience is that we value money only when our deep values are not being met. If our deep values are met while making the wages of a childcare worker, then I suspect we would find ourselves happy with our work, regardless of what we might have thought about the importance of money beforehand. Conversely, no matter how much we are paid, if our core values are not being met then we are likely to see ourselves as underpaid.

Experience

So far, we have discussed abilities, interests, and values. Each of these represents an important component of our good work. Finally, I think we need to look at what we have already done, our experience. While what we have done is no sure sign of what we *can* do, or what we *should* do, it is a good indication – sometimes positive, sometimes negative – of both.

If my high school guidance counselor had asked me what I had experience doing, he would have found that what I had done was build houses. This was a requirement of growing up in the family home. Dad built a new house every year or two and we kids were required to participate. It was how we earned summer income, but more than that, it was a part of family life. So very early I learned to work with cement, to hammer a nail properly, to lay out a wall, and to put up wallboard. With that small bit of information the counselor could have gained tremendous insight into why I considered architecture, and into what I could do. Then he could have asked, "Did you enjoy what you did?" (an open question). If I had been honest, I would have said no, I hated it. That would have been a good caution around the architecture, and perhaps opened the door to a larger conversation about what kinds of things I had done which I enjoyed.

It does not take too many years of activity, at home, at school, in the community, or in the workplace, to establish very important patterns. Imagine someone who has operated a dry-cleaning business, managed a ball team, taken regular vacations with his family, and attended church every Sunday. In this mythical person we see energy around the poles of family, community, stability, and spirituality. If he were to consider making a career shift, it is unlikely that he should take up work on an off-shore oil rig. More appropriate alternatives might include the operation of a sporting goods store, or perhaps a religious goods store. Or consider someone who "temps" as an administrative assistant, does lots of free-lance graphic design, has maintained no long-term relationships, and enjoys mountain biking. Here energy is transient, perhaps highly creative, and tied to nature. For her, career alternatives are unlikely to involve a long-term job and a life in the suburbs. Alternatives might relate to environmental initiatives or multi-media work.

In each case, what the person has done provides important clues as to what they should do.

Getting Started

As is probably obvious by now, searching for our soul work, our good work is no easy thing. One of the hopeful things about this process is that the fundamentals of who we are – our capabilities, our potential, and our deep values – do not change that much. Of course we grow and mature, but who we are when we enter the working world is not a lot different from who we are when we leave.

This next section builds upon our understanding of ourselves in order to give some guidance for career planning. It is for those who are in the midst of a career transition and looking for direction. If this does not describe you, you may wish to skip ahead to the next chapter.

Step One: Determine Your Abilities

Career changes open up the door to any one of the more than 20,000 career alternatives. That means you must take a careful look back to see what abilities you have demonstrated in the past. This does not mean you will necessarily use all of those abilities, but you will need to identify your abilities in order to move into any new career.

In order to identify your abilities, do the following exercise. First, you need several pages of blank paper. Across the top of one write, "home." Across the top of another write, "present job." Across the others write, "recreation," "past jobs," "community," "volunteer," "church," or "hobbies" as appropriate. Then take each sheet in turn and list in single words or short phrases the tasks you carry out in each one. For example, "organize weekly menu" might fall on the "home page." On the "present job" page you might list, "organize staff meetings," "stay up to date on current software," or "manage 70-customer sales route." Do this for every page until you have an exhaustive list of your abilities.

This can be a long process and you may not be able to complete it on the first attempt. As I said earlier, each of us has hundreds of abilities. But eventually, you will reach the point where nothing more comes to mind.

These lists contain the things you do. It is unlikely this is the full range of your abilities. Most of us have untapped abilities, abilities we have never had the opportunity to use, or develop. However, everything on these lists is something you know you can do and supports your intention to change careers.

Now go back to those lists with a highlighter, or a pen of another color. In some way, identify any ability you have been recognized for. This recognition may have come in the form of an off-hand comment by a co-worker, or it may have come as a formal award. Regardless, these probably represent your strongest abilities. While they may not form the basis of your new career, they are the areas in which you stand out and they should be taken very seriously as you make your plans.

Do not be surprised if the abilities which you think are most significant don't show up on the "present job" sheet. For many people, our outstanding abilities show up in the other parts of our lives, and not on the job. This is, by itself, a good reason to consider changing careers. When we have found our good work, we tend to discover either new significant abilities, or that our past significant abilities are being put to good use.

At this point you have taken stock of what you have to offer. To obtain your good work will require you make use of many of your abilities, and now you know what they (presently) are.

Step Two: Determine Your Interests

Now take your lists and run through them again with a different agenda. This time you are looking for the things you *enjoy* doing. With another color, or in some other way, identify everything on your lists of abilities which you *like to do*.

The emphasis here is on *what you do* or *have done*, because what we *actually do* is a far better indicator of who we are than what we *think* we would enjoy doing, what we think it is *appropriate* for us to enjoy, or what we would like others to *believe* we enjoy.

I confess that when I drive the company car I always have the radio tuned to a loud rock and roll station, but when I leave the car I am usually careful to tune it to a classical music station. The *real* me enjoys something quite different from the impression I sometimes try to leave. So be honest about what you enjoy. (You can always destroy the list later if it is too incriminating.)

Now that you have highlighted those items on your list which are most satisfying, the abilities of which you are most proud or where you find the most pleasure, look for themes, anything which stands out as recurring.

When I look at the list I have made, a couple of things stand out which I expected. A lot of what I am proud of involves creating and developing. Another thing which turns up is the prevalence of words, both spoken and written. Curiously, although I do not think of myself as a teacher, a lot of what I enjoy doing involves instructing in one setting or another.

Another thing which stands out is that despite my intellectual interest in things spiritual, very little shows up on my list of interests which would indicate that. I do not particularly enjoy meditating, praying, or any of the other spiritual disciplines. (In fact I tend to avoid them.) Now, either this means that I am not *really* interested in things spiritual or, as I believe is the case, spirituality runs deeply through my interests in ways which are non-traditional (part of why I am writing this book).

As you can see, when we look at our interests, we begin a dialogue with ourselves which helps us to see who we are and where we would like to go. But it is important at this point not to draw too many conclusions. Our interests are important, vitally so, but they are not the heart of the matter. They get us looking in the right direction, but we have more steps to take on our journey. Put your interests aside for now. We will come back to them.

Step Three: Determine Your Deep Values

This step takes us heartward, into the core of our being, into the stuff we live and breathe and of which we are made. This is not an easy step. Apart from those values we share with our fellow human beings, our deep values do not usually declare themselves easily. Sometimes we find things which trouble us deeply. Sometimes we find contradictions between our deep values. Sometimes we do not have enough experience to make clear what our deep values are.

We know that for each of us, the ability to maintain our lives is a deep value. This drives us to work. However, there are times when "maintenance" is not good enough, and we are willing to put off or sacrifice our well-being for other deep values. We need not concern ourselves here with these times, except to note that if there is something we are certain we would sacrifice our lives for, we can list it as a deep value.

The real difficulty is discovering those deep values which are unique to us. To know ourselves well is as much a gift as an accomplishment. This knowledge is often born only out of long suffering. Our deep values surface most clearly under great stress. It is when we are pushed by the world around us that we find ourselves saying, "Here I stand." We also start looking inward for resources and strengths we previously never used or were not aware we had. These resources and strengths often show us that our unconscious has been hard at work on important things which have never before made it to the light.

Being fired from my job, a job I loved and at which I thought I was doing good work, was gruesomely painful. It took place over three months and included betrayal by folks whom I had trusted. It is not an uncommon story. What I found amazing in the process, both at the time and in retrospect, was how I continued to do my work during that time. My values were put to the test and by the end I knew things about myself which I did not know before.

First, I found out how important my family was to me. As with many professional men, I had invested too much of my identity in my job and not enough in my marriage and family. (In some measure that is still true, but I know now which way I will jump if I am forced.) Second, I discovered how much concern I have with personal integrity. As one who has worked with large bureaucracies, I have grown used to bending the rules, even violating them entirely if that is what the job required. And yet, when the pressure is on, I do not hide and I am quite prepared to stand up and say what I have done and why. I treasure the opportunity to be clear and direct, vulnerable with regard to goals and methods. The third thing I found out was that I was prepared to be emotionally destroyed in order to see that good things came of the firing process for those who remained behind. To some degree, I valued their potential more than my own health.

At this point, I know that my deep values include family, the meaning of "everything," community well-being, and walking in faithfulness to my God. Not one of those deep values surfaced easily. I suspect I will find more as I age and as life continues to throw big events at me. The death of my father taught me many things. My marriage has taught me more. But I have been spared many of those things which other people face and which cause their deep values to surface. For example, no war or political catastrophe has driven me from my home, causing me to rethink what home really means.

There are many events and situations which push us into the realm of our deep values. For most of us, these are the only way we encounter these values. However, there are others of us who know what counts almost from birth. Some of us are gifted with flashes of insight along the way. Regardless of when or how we learn them, our deep values are the unshakable pillars of our being.

Here is a series of exercises to help you grapple with your deep values.

Let's start with a visualization exercise. First, quiet yourself. Now imagine yourself walking through your home. As you enter each room, stop and remember significant experiences you have had there. Try to experience the emotions and feelings that come from being in each room. Think about what *values* might be associated with these feelings. When you have gone through all the rooms in your house, ask yourself if there was anything missing. Are there rooms your house does not have, but that you wish it did? Ask yourself what values might be associated with these "new" rooms.

Here is another visualization experience you can try. Quiet yourself and imagine each deep value dropping into a pool inside you, a dark, deep, cool pool in some inner chasm, the pool of your soul. Some of the values may float at the surface, waiting to be skimmed off, indicating they are not the key to your soul. Some might sink into the water, comfortable, indicating they are part of your soul's home. Others might become the water, indicating that they are critical to your identity.

Once you have some idea of what your deep values are, write them on a piece of paper (in a column down the middle). Around them list your interests. Draw strong lines between your interests and the values they reflect (an interest can reflect more than one value). Draw a box around interests which do not seem to have a great deal of connection to your values (these can be disregarded). Now circle any clusters of interests and values which seem to belong together. If all goes well, you should have one or more clusters which indicate where the most important parts of your life come together. These clusters are the keys to your good work.

Next comes research. Try listing possible occupations which might go with each cluster. This can be a tentative or speculative list. Once you have a few, start talking to people in those occupations. Find out what they do, how they got there, and what they think of their work. Check career resources for other related occupations (these should also list typical skills and training necessary for these fields of work). Volunteer if you can, or work with someone in an area related to one of your clusters. Ask if you can "shadow" someone for a day or a week to find out what their work really looks like. This research will also allow you to list the skills necessary for the work and compare that to the skills you already have. This may indicate that you have the skills you need, or that you need to obtain more. If so, you can begin to do what it takes to obtain those skills, either through schooling or some form of training.

Step Four: Evaluate Your Experience

Much of what is usually considered experience has already been dealt with in step one, "Determine your abilities." What we have *not* considered to this point, and what we are looking at here, is *how* and *where* you obtained those abilities.

Return to your lists of abilities. These have already been separated into categories which roughly correspond to *where* you obtained them. Now list the job titles, or the names of the day-to-day roles through which you obtained them. Put these titles and names in chronological order, or if that is not easy to do, because they overlap, then do the following: On the left side of the page, put a series of marks, one for every five years of age, spaced an inch or so apart. Then, in the open page to the right of the marks, write each title or name in the place vertically corresponding to when you started. Then draw a line down the page from the title corresponding to how long the title or name applied. This could be a very short or a very long line. Each subsequent title or name will move to the right of the previous one, allowing room for a clear line to be drawn below without overlap. When you are done, you should have a chronological "map" of your experience.

Now ask yourself, "Are there any patterns here?" Many people find that when a job changes, many other roles in their lives change at the same time. Others find that when something happens that changes their values, it will show up as a series of changes in their jobs and other roles.

Also ask yourself, "Do any of these titles or names reflect my interests and values?" They may or they may not. It *does* happen that who we are and what we genuinely value find little expression in our life, but it can also be a sign that we are not who we think we are, or that there are other issues we need to resolve. Personal issues, family issues, and that whole host of emotional issues each one of us carries around, can have a profound impact on why we do what we do.

Where past titles or roles *do* reflect your interests and values, ask yourself, "How did I move into that job or role?" How you answer this question says a lot about how you do the practical work of *finding* your good work. Some of us make careful choices, and others of us work by intuition. Still others find it is a combination of both, with perhaps some chance thrown into it. While you do not have to continue to use your previous method of finding work, it is important to identify it before proceeding.

Experience is *not* the most important thing about us, certainly not as important as abilities, interests, and values, but it can say something to us about who we are. As we pursue our good work, our experience is an important indicator of how far we have come toward finding our good work.

Step Five: Evaluate Your Training

Up to this point I have not mentioned training. This is not because I think training is unimportant. It *is* important. But training is a secondary part of finding your good work. The soul gives direction, and then we add the training. And then we retrain. Training must be lifelong if we are to cope with the changes occurring in the world around us, but it is a minor part of the quest for our good work.

I constantly hear references to training as if it were the solution to *every* problem, even spiritual problems. Training, or so it seems, will give us direction, provide us with wealth, build us a place of esteem in the community, supply us with the tools to contribute, solve the deficit, and find us our proper place in life. Not true. Unfortunately, I risk sounding like a lunatic when I say this, but training which is not wise to who we are leads us astray. We need training which works *with* us, providing us with the skills we need, and in keeping with our deep values.

But before I look at how the skills we learn through training can reflect our deep values, it is important that we learn which skills are necessary, regardless. Training in these skills is essential, whether we learn them at home, on the job, or in school. They are as important to us in our culture as knowledge of edible plants is for a Bushman. There is very little good work to be found when we are unable to cope effectively with our day-to-day circumstances.

The following list of necessary skills reflects the changes happening in the global economy and in the nature of work itself. The driving forces behind the changes necessitating these skills are computerization, massive information flow, and human global interconnection. There are many books which examine these forces and why they have the training consequences they do, and I only touch upon them here to ensure that while we pursue our good work, we do not neglect the basics of survival.

At this point, it is clear that all of us need seven sets of skills related to effective work in the contemporary economy. Some of these are easily obtained, and most of them are skills we will already have.

LITERACY, NUMERIC ABILITY, AND BASIC COMPUTER FAMILIARITY

Basic reading, writing, addition, subtraction, multiplication, and keyboard facility are essentials for most working environments. While it is possible to still find workplaces where these are not necessary, the number is shrinking all the time. Computerization has meant that even the most routine jobs usually require the ability to read and write, to understand numbers and perform simple calculations, and to enter the information in a computer through a keyboard.

PEOPLE MANAGEMENT SKILLS

In the information age, all jobs are becoming people jobs where orders are not so much given and received, but relationships developed. The most critical relationships are those with customers and these relationships require tact, good judgment, and a pleasant manner. Team-based management requires these plus excellent delegation, empowerment, and group organization skills.

COMMUNICATION SKILLS

Being able to communicate information is absolutely essential. This means understanding what information is required and knowing how to present it orally, in writing, or in a presentation. Good listening skills are part and parcel of this.

RESEARCH SKILLS

Knowing what information is needed, finding out where it is located, and then getting it involves a major set of skills. These skills can be as simple as knowing when to phone a supplier and what to ask, or as complex as collecting a sophisticated set of parameters for a proposal. This used to be the job of middle management, but middle management is disappearing as fast as computers can be dropped onto desk tops, into warehouses, and within equipment. Now everyone needs to know how to do some research.

TIME AND RESOURCE MANAGEMENT SKILLS

The ability to plan a day and organize activities in order to achieve goals is not yet essential, but it is becoming routine in much work. Even clerical staff are being forced to be "self-starters." Eventually, I suspect, we will all need to be able to assess resources – be they time, money, paper, computer access, trucks, staff, whatever – and decide how to best apply them to the tasks at hand.

CRITICAL THINKING AND JUDGMENT FORMATION SKILLS

The ability to follow orders has been the key to success since the industrial revolution. Doing what you were told was the order of the day. An acquaintance who once worked in lower management in a bank, back in the days before computers, tells of having all of his activities written out for him on a sheet of paper taped to his desktop. He did what was on the list and *only* what was on the list.

Now, in most industries, front line workers are given control of a wide range of tasks. This means that more of us are required to think well about what should happen next. We need to be able to decide what is within and outside of our scope (and therefore when to refer to others), which policies apply, and which systems will be most effective.

OPPORTUNITY AWARENESS AND DEVELOPMENT SKILLS

It is a changing world and so we need always to be looking for the next change to hit our work. Ideally, we learn to anticipate which changes will be necessary and to institute them *before* they are required. At the very least, we need to ensure that our systems maintain flexibility and that we know how to respond to change when it arrives. This applies to both employers and employees.

GRAPHIC DESIGN

Graphic design is the eighth item on my list of seven. While I have yet to see this item on anyone else's list, I am adding it to my own. In my experience, if you work in an office or information intensive environment and you do not know the basics of page layout, you are in trouble.

* * *

You can pick up the above skills in many different ways and formal education is only one. You can set out to learn them through life activities. You can include them in your on-the-job training. You can sign up for seminars. You can enroll in a Bachelor of Arts degree program.

(Here again, I realize that I am bucking an educational trend to technical specialization and science degrees, but most of these skills are basic to any good liberal arts degree, and some, like critical thinking and judgment formation skills, are rarely taught outside one. Of course, a liberal arts degree does not guarantee the ability to think critically and a science degree does not rule it out, but there is no question in my mind that a B.A. is by far the better degree for teaching people to be effective as thinkers and as leaders. This claim is supported by both anecdotal evidence and research which Simon Fraser University has done on its own grads.)

Another great place to learn many of these skills is in the home. Anyone who can manage a household of working adults and school age children already possesses many of these critical skills. Still another way to learn these skills is as a volunteer. Volunteers are often allowed access to responsibilities and opportunities they would have little chance of being given in a workplace (responsibility and opportunity are the only form of pay many volunteers get). A hospital visitation program teaches tremendous people relations and communication skills. Boy Scout coordinators learn management, resource development, people, and communication skills. There are, in short, many, many ways to acquire the basic survival skills of the contemporary workplace.

Then there are the specific skills you need to do your particular good work. These skills are as individual as the task ahead of you. The training you need is the training which will allow you access to the positions, resources, and opportunities which will allow you to do that work. This *may* include training in a specific technical skill set, particular to the work itself. But it can also be much broader than that. For example, if you discover that your good work involves healing people, then you need training which will allow you to do this. This may include training in any of a variety of traditional or nontraditional medical professions. But you will also need training in skills which allow you to do more than "fix" bodies according to prescription. You need to learn the skills of seeing truth and of listening honestly. You must know what else is happening in the field, what other disciplines might work well with yours.

Finally, there are the skills you need to stay in touch with your soul. These are the disciplines which keep you in touch with your deep values in the midst of the rush and bustle of everyday life. I will be discussing these in some detail in chapter six, so will only list a few of them here.

They can include flash prayers, devotional practices, centering exercises, visualization exercises, meditation, and the practice of silence.

While anyone can learn and practice these disciplines on their own, it is often helpful to work with a spiritual director. These people often work in the context of a religious retreat center. Retreat centers can be found in most cities, large or small, across the country. Even though they are usually run by a particular religious denomination, such as the United, Anglican, or Roman Catholic Church, almost all of them will be open to receiving guests from any Christian tradition. There are also increasing numbers of retreat centers which represent the other great world religions, including Buddhist, Baha'i, and even aboriginal traditions.

Mentors also play a key role in the teaching of spiritual disciplines, as do the communities we are a part of (more on community and mentors later in this chapter).

Step Six: Find Resources

Despite the myth of our age that we, as individuals, can do everything on our own, in fact we cannot. We will need help to find our good work. We have work to do, and this work, like all work, requires resources. These resources can include people, books, or other materials. Consider using any or all of the following.

NOVELS AND MOVIES

Fiction has lost its place of grace in our culture. Entertainment is what we call it, but we miss a larger truth when we do so. Any well written story carries to us intimations of truth. In each character, we find spirits at work, spirits we can learn from.

The easiest way to use a story is as a contrast with our own life. We can replay for ourselves what is happening in the story and try on the various roles. In our agreement or disagreement with what we observe, we will find ourselves revealed and spiritual guidance given. This may not uncover our specific good work, but it will help reveal our deep values and push us on.

Of all contemporary authors, Andrew Greeley, the Roman Catholic priest and sociologist, seems to me to have caught in his novels the urban struggle for soul most thoroughly. While I suspect that his books will not become classics, they provoke much thought about the way God finds us in this world. Many Science Fiction authors push us to consider who we are and who we might become. William Gibson paints particular, disturbing pictures of the future, but his characters are all possessed of an integrity and possibility which says something positive about what we can achieve, regardless of the technology and social forces in which we are caught. Most mysteries play out the drama of redemption through self-sacrifice.

Film, too, can push us along. My personal complaint is that we confuse "glitz" with "deep," and that regardless, Hollywood has a terrible time grappling with reality, let alone spirituality. Still, there are gems out there, and not all film comes from Hollywood.

CLASSICS AND SACRED SCRIPTURES

A classic is a story which resonates as true over a long period of time. At some level, a classic speaks to us of what it is that is important about life. (When it fails to do so, it loses its status as a classic.) By reading and watching classics, we get caught up in a story which brings us closer to who we are as human beings and where we should be going. Sacred scriptures are particularly important in this process – whether it is the Bible, the Upanishads, or some other sacred text you read.

Unfortunately, few classics have concerned themselves with work as we understand it today. In part this is because the economy in which we work is a radically new invention. However, *human beings* have not changed that much, nor have our deep values, so the classics can still be excellent resources.

SELF-HELP BOOKS

There are many good self-help books. Libraries and book stores are full of them. Regardless of where you are on the journey, you are likely to find some assistance. This is one of the few places where people have taken work seriously and have tried to explore what it means for human well-being.

COURSES

Most communities offer courses on career-planning basics. If they are any good, they will push past the surface and ask some of the deeper questions. I encourage you to ask at the local college or university counseling department. They may not offer anything, but they should know who does.

By this point you will have recognized a shortage of material which relates specifically to work and the soul. We are at the cutting edge of a revolution, and with the exception of the self-help section of the bookstore, not many parts of our society have begun to respond adequately.

Step Seven: Find Community

I am convinced that no journey of the soul belongs to the individual alone. We must travel *together* or not travel at all. I cannot imagine how we can find our good work without having others with whom we can share the stories of our struggle, and who can offer support and encouragement. As I reflect on my own journeying, I know that genuine progress has always taken place in the context of a supportive community. Sometimes that community was invisible to me at the time, but looking back I can see it clearly.

In retrospect, the significance of community stands out for me in one of my most important transitions. Back when I finished my first graduate degree and was trying to discover what to do with the rest of my life I felt completely alone. Admittedly, I was already married, and changing the diapers on a newborn. But I remember standing in the middle of the street in front of our apartment in a rundown part of the city, on a winter afternoon, and looking around with a sense of near complete desolation. I had no idea what to do, where to go, where to turn. I remember saying to myself, "If I am still here a year from now, I will give up."

But I was not alone. I had a mentor, though I did not consider him that at the time. I had friends who cared, even though I did not feel close to them. I knew I had a good education, even if I had no idea how to use it. And, totally unknown to me, in another country (at another school) there was a group of people who knew about me and who were doing their best to help me.

I was not living in that apartment a year later, and things changed very profoundly for me, due almost entirely to an invisible community of support and concern. Yes, I made decisions in that time, important decisions, but the outcomes were due to the work of a body of people whom I still count as friends.

So how does one go about finding a community of companions? I am aware of at least three ways to find a community if you do not already have one. The first and most obvious way is to intentionally join an already existing community, such as a church or religious community, a service club, or some other neighborhood association. The second way is through service. By serving in some capacity, by working to improve the situation of others, by giving of what you have, you take a significant step toward community. The third way involves vulnerability, as you open yourself to others, become honest with them, and reveal your weak points and your hurts. Once again, self-help or religious groups can be a *safe* place to try these latter two suggestions. But *any* community group, collective organization, or community initiative, can provide the context.

MENTORS

A special part of any community are its mentors. Someone who takes a special interest in your journey and who can guide you is a tremendous gift. A number of people have been mentors to me. What strikes me about each is that they could see more potential in me than I could see in myself. They were considerably older than I. Perhaps this is what we need in a mentor, someone older who sees our potential, and someone who can steer us in directions we have trouble understanding. In my case, these situations of guidance took place on an occasional basis, but others may want to meet regularly with a mentor.

I also believe that mentors are not nearly as scarce in reality as they often seem. I suspect that there are more wise people willing to offer help than there are those willing to be helped. Perhaps this is due, once again, to the myth that we must make it on our own, or perhaps we need training in order to see and use mentors. Regardless, they are there, and rarely more than a request for advice away.

Step Eight: Know in Your Heart

This sounds straightforward, but it is not. On the one hand, I believe that when we have found our good work we experience a resonance inside us that says we are home. I believe it, because that is what I have felt. On the other hand, each of us is capable of deceiving ourselves profoundly both into feeling what is *not* there, or into not feeling what *is* there. I conclude from this that we must know in our heart *and* be affirmed by our community.

If someone came to me and said, "I know this is what I am supposed to do with my life, but everyone around me says I am crazy," I would be suspicious. I would want to know a great deal more before agreeing (or disagreeing). More often I see that when we have genuinely found the time-space for our good work, those around us accept it. There is both an internal and external inevitability about it. Our inner voice will resonate not only with our tasks, but with outer voices as well.

Still, this does not mean we will *never* hear objections, and stories certainly exist of people who have found their good work and who have rightly affirmed it over the protests of their communities.

When I found my calling, it was with a profound "Ah ha!" and I had tears in my eyes. Others recognized that calling as well. If they had not, and other circumstances had not combined to reinforce that calling, I would be prepared to think I had been mistaken.

But that has not happened. Instead my path, regardless of how it has twisted and turned, has reinforced for me the knowledge of what I am to do. I believe we can each achieve this same place where, in our hearts, we know what our good work is to be.

Step Nine: Get Going

It may not seem to make sense to include a section on getting started in a larger section on the same theme. By now, everything should have added up to a whole range of ideas and plans. All we have to do is start with step one and proceed. However, my reason for including this section is to suggest the opposite. I want to discourage you from proceeding immediately.

Exploring our good work is serious business and we are not always ready to proceed. Sometimes we have other life issues which we need to deal with first.

Also recognize that this task is not for the fainthearted. Finding your good work can be a very lengthy process, with some difficult passages. If all is relatively well now, then it may be that you are in the right place at the moment.

When the time comes to proceed you will know it. Usually, when we are prepared to make the necessary changes, things begin to change of their own accord. Then it is often a matter of hanging on tight as our life takes off on its own.

Finally, remember that as long as you work with honesty and integrity to find your good work, in some measure you will already be doing it. The journey itself is as important as the outcome, and the path of the good is always open for those who genuinely seek it.

5

Next Steps: Reengineering as a Spiritual Discipline

Not long ago, I talked to a small business owner who reflected on his progress over the life of his business. He said that he can still remember the day he signed his first contract for more than $100,000. It seemed absolutely momentous, and worth every effort to achieve it. He put in long hours to make it happen. Then he told me about his most recent contract, worth $6 million. He put in long hours to make that happen too, thinking of the 60 jobs on the line, and the long-term worth of the company. He mused, "Now I hardly look at anything under $500,000. It doesn't seem worth the effort. Sometimes I wonder what will be worth the effort after I sign a $10 million contract, or a $20 million contract?"

Then he talked about how he gets so caught up in each new achievement, and how after he makes the deal, nothing has *really* improved. In fact, in some parts of his life, things may have become worse. A big contract can take him three months of 60- to 70-hour weeks to set up, weeks which leave him completely exhausted. Yet at the end of it, once he has the deal, he recognizes that he has almost missed everything that has happened in his family for those three months. He says at that point he needs to spend time carefully with his partner and children so that he can reestablish his ties with them.

That businessman is more honest than many. The social worker who takes calls every weekend from clients, the teacher who spends evenings and weekends grading papers, the many who spend far too much time with their (important) work and too little time with their families and communities, are all too common. And we tend to reward them. Our whole culture seems to conspire to reward overwork and blindness to the big picture. Honesty about what we have to gain and what we have to lose by this behavior is something we desperately need.

My businessman friend knows he could work a 70-hour week, every week of the year, and sometimes he is tempted to do so. He has a reputation for running an organization that turns out excellent work and he knows that there is a far larger market for his product than he has tapped to date. But what holds him back is the recognition that to pursue those possibilities, to turn his organization into a $100-million-a-year outfit, would cost first his relationships, then his health. Presently, he has an informal agreement with his family that he only puts his efforts into one or two major new clients per year. That agreement is not easy for him to live by, but it helps him keep what is genuinely important in mind.

He may never make the Fortune 500 with his company, or be recognized as a great business leader, but he *will* be remembered by his family. His community will remember his work on various boards and with non-profits. His employees will remember him as a man who modeled both good work and a good life. These achievements are perhaps not what they *could* be, not the type that will get him untold wealth or media recognition, but they are what they *should be.*

Reengineering

This man has begun to spiritually reengineer his work. The term itself comes from the business world. According to its main guru, Michael Hammer, and described in any one of his books, a new way of understanding work must be found which will create the efficient and quick-response organizations today's economy calls for. Specifically, reengineering refers to a radical change in the way things are done, a change which focuses on *processes* rather than on *tasks.* In other words, the *place* to start is with the big "hows" of business. And the *way* to start is with a blank piece of paper; we need to throw out our old assumptions and start over.

While not all business concepts are equally useful to the individual, what Hammer says about reengineering is true for businesses and individuals alike. When we look at our work, at what we do and what it means, we really have to start over. We need to throw out our assumptions that work is about pay, about careers, about doing tasks, and about getting ready to stop working. We must find a new vision of what we are trying to achieve, a vision which will leave us certain that what we are doing is good work.

The question is, "What does it mean to reengineer our work?" Reengineering is, as I have said, a term from the business world, a world which still focuses on profit and loss, not one which seeks wholeness and well-being. What does it mean for us, as individuals with soul, to take on this challenge? How does this concept relate to good work?

The essence of reengineering, according to Hammer, is its emphasis on *process.* Our old assumption, he says, is that work is a series of tasks. We have things to do, and tools and methods we have learned to do them with. We take these tools and methods and use them in tiny pieces, over and over, until our work is done. It does not matter if the work is brain surgery or washing the kitchen floor, we all follow the same set of operational assumptions.

Here is how it works: When I sit in front of my computer (where I do most of my work) I have a list of things I want to accomplish. My "To Do" list usually includes a set of tasks like, "complete PBT proposal, phone Joe regarding pricing on new printer, check program outcomes with John, outline next chapter, ask Christine about problem client and get documentation..." It often runs to 15 or more items. Some are marked urgent. Some sit at the bottom of the list for days (and sometimes weeks) on end, waiting for me to get to them. But regardless, they are all specific tasks and I get great satisfaction from ticking them off the list when they are done. To do them, I apply specific, learned skills, more or less well. This is my work. It is also the way *many* of us work. Getting those tasks done is what we try to achieve.

But if I stop and look at this from Hammer's point of view, I am fundamentally mistaken about what it is that I am doing. It is not that those specific tasks are unimportant; the problem is that the perspective I bring to them is fundamentally mistaken. I need to step back from those tasks and think about what I am trying to accomplish in terms of the big picture. It may be that in my emphasis on specific tasks, and what I have to do, I have missed the point of my work.

Reengineering suggests that what I *should* be doing is getting back to the basic stuff that leads me to do this work in the first place. I should be asking, why are these things on my list? What am I trying to accomplish, not just today, but with this work situation? How can I go about regrasping what is important and what is secondary in order to get satisfaction, not from little ticks on a list, but from knowing that what I have done is a meaningful part of what my life is about? Where do they fit in the big picture?

The Person Inside the Worker

Good work does not come naturally. If it did the world would not look like it does (and books like this would not need to be written). Good work is something which takes effort to find and effort to do; and that effort must be backed by skill and discipline. Yet even more, good work must be supported by a vision. This is where reengineering helps us. Reengineering helps us gain a vision for how we can become not just better workers, but renewed and renewing workers. As we take on this challenge, not only do *we* change, we change the *world*.

My assumption, at this point, is that the area of work you are doing is one where you feel comfortable, that there is something about what you do and its outcomes which resonates with who you believe you are, that your work reflects your values, and that your work builds upon your skills. It need not be work which you think of as your "calling," but before you begin to reengineer, you *do* need to make sure that the first step is not to change your career track. (While we can come to the conclusion, once we have tried to reengineer, that we should have been trying it elsewhere, it does not make a lot of sense to put out the effort when you know you are in the wrong place to begin with.) The beginning point must be a sense that the work in front of you is important to you.

With that clear, our task is to take this business concept and use it to pry open our inner world of work, grab hold of the basics, and perform a fundamental shift. Reengineering is the conceptual tool we use to bring us in touch with what counts in work, and to guide us through this stage on the journey.

The essence of reengineering is its focus on process. Of course, every process is linked to every other process and it gets very hard to know the precise boundaries of each. *Our* work is affected by the work of *others*. What we experience at *work* affects how we feel at *home*, and vice versa. So too, some work processes run through a number of days or weeks. Other projects or processes will last a few months. Still others will wrap up in a matter of hours. A book project such as this one, may last years from conception to completion. In other words, there are many processes and many *types* of processes in our lives, and each one could be the basis for reengineering. So where do we start?

Home and Work

I think it helps to remember at this point that good work involves the deep or core structures of my life. Many of the processes I have named change, but what does not change is the movement I make from being with my family, to immersing myself in my work, to returning to my family. How well I manage that process, and what goes on in the midst of it, makes all the difference, long after all the other projects and processes have come and gone. It is also the size of process I can understand, evaluate, and change. While it may be appropriate to change my whole working life, that is too big a process to get hold of easily. I want to deal with a unit of my life which makes discreet sense. So for now, the process of getting from home to work and back again is the one we will look at.

Home is where our work starts and where it ends. Home is also the place from which to examine the outcome of our work. How we walk in the door at the end of the shift, at the end of the day, or after returning from a trip, is the real measure of the process. Who we are, and what we bring with us, are the truly important outcomes. Life partners, children, community, and friends are all deeply concerned with this outcome. This is where the real experience of work comes to rest.

This is easy to see in retrospect, but hard to see (I think particularly for men) before you come to this conclusion. One of the basic strategies we take, when dealing with our lives, is to put our work life before our home life.

There are those of us in specific fields who have particular trouble with this. Business leaders and those in the helping professions are especially misled. The work itself seems so important, either the dollar figures are so high, or the outcomes so critical, that any effort seems worth it, regardless of its impact on home and family. As well, we tend to measure our lives by promotions, pay rates, tasks, and job titles. All these things have a profound impact on the way we see ourselves.

The problem is, of course, that the way most of us are remembered after we are dead is not by our job description or total tonnage moved, our sales record or size of caseload managed. We are remembered for the way we have treated our friends and family, for the contribution we have made to the community outside of our work. The important outcomes of our work are at home and in the community, not in the tasks and responsibilities of the work, no matter how important we think those tasks happen to be.

But the questions remain: What should the outcomes be? What do our families and communities want from us? Who do *we* need to be at the end of our work? These are not easy questions to answer, because we are now dealing with a complex accumulation of genuine and felt needs, both our own and those of the people around us. Still, despite the differences among us, there are certain characteristic wants and needs most of us share and which our work either provides for or impacts upon.

First, work meets our *maintenance* needs; it is the source of the income with which we provide food and shelter for ourselves and for those close to us. Our maintenance needs are absolutely essential. They have been the key driver of employment throughout human history, and still are in many cultures around the world today. To provide the two basics of food and shelter we will work long and hard.

Despite a common perception to the contrary, *maintenance* is no longer the dominant reason those of us in the middle class work. While it is *a* reason we work, if we were prepared to live at 1960s standards of living, we could cut our time on the job by two thirds to one half of our present working hours (and eliminate unemployment at the same time).

However, must of us are not satisfied with *maintaining* our lives. We constantly want to improve the quality of our existence. We never seem to have enough. That brings us to the second thing work provides us – *luxury*. Many of us travel the world. Most of us live in large, warm, well-lit homes. We are entertained lavishly. We eat exotic food. And it is never enough. We want more and better, and more and better for our kids and our community. So we work ever harder and more productively to supply it. The desire for luxury is an extremely powerful motivator.

The third thing work brings us is a sense of *meaning* and *self-esteem*. I believe our work is driven as much by our desire to do something *meaningful for ourselves*, as it is driven by our need for food and shelter, or our powerful desire for luxury. We gain much of our identity and many opportunities to express ourselves productively through our work.

When we put these three together, we can say that the process of moving from home to work and back again is driven by the need for food and shelter, the desire for luxury, and the need for meaning and self-esteem. These are the things we want to have satisfied when we come back in the door after our hours of work. Of course, each of us has other, individual drives as well, but these are the ones most of us share. These are also the guides to reengineering our work. Having identified these common outcomes, we can look at what we do, and how we do it.

Reengineering for Maintenance

When we look at our day-to-day work as a process with the goal of providing the basics of human life – food, clothing, and shelter – it is obvious that the process works extremely well. Not only do we provide those for ourselves, but through our income taxes we also provide those for the orphan, the sick, and the poor. Work does what it is supposed to do and so effectively that there are few in North America who do not have access to those essentials.* It is hard to imagine how we can address this process in such a way as to do better.

The one issue here is collective. While our individual work does an excellent job of providing for our basic needs, our increasing productivity in the workplace places large numbers of people at risk of losing their jobs. I have no doubt that the future holds more work dislocations than the past or the present. Economic turbulence is almost certain to increase, and a higher level of permanent unemployment is quite possible. When that is combined with a

---

*This does not preclude the very real issues of homelessness, malnutrition, and poverty, from which far too many people suffer. These issues are complex and *not* tied to the ability of our work to take care of everyone. As one who has worked in social services for years, I believe that these issues are not resolved only by tax expenditures (though these are essential, and should probably increase), but need to be addressed at the same time through changes in social values and much more work on mental health care and the creation of more and better work opportunities for those with a wide range of disabilities.

reduction in our collective will to care for those who are hurt by the turbulence, through reductions in Employment Insurance and in welfare payments, we face a situation where for some people the process needs to change. For them, the outcome of our work is suffering and the risk of losing the basics. When our work contributes to the loss of the basics for others, it has gone wrong. Work that destroys work for others is never good work.

Still, it is hard at this point to imagine a more effective process for producing the basics than the one we presently have.

Reengineering for Luxury

The idea that we want more luxury strikes most of us as repulsive, so we phrase it in the language of need: the kids need a bigger back yard to play in, we need to get away on a vacation to Mexico to recover, we need to get a Ph.D. to advance (my pet need), or we need a new car because the one we have is getting old. The reality is that these "needs" have very little to do with any need ever imagined by most human beings throughout human history. We are deeply committed to living in luxury, and we will sacrifice a great deal of our time and energy in its pursuit.

No matter how repulsive the idea, we need to face our desire for luxury. We will not achieve well-being if we skim over troubling areas with platitudes, and luxury is extremely important to us. Luxury is deeply engrained with the "what" and "why" of our work. I would not want to be the one to come home one day and say that my work would no longer be used to support all the luxuries my family has become used to. There would be a terrible scene, one that would raise all the basic issues of family life. Luxury is a deep concern, and it is an outcome of our day-to-day work.

When it comes to luxury, our situation is ambiguous. If we measure our luxury by the standard of kings of a century ago, we have succeeded beyond their wildest dreams. However, if we measure our luxury by the standard of our neighbors, then we fall short. I have met very few people who were not deeply envious of the luxury of someone else, and willing to work very hard to obtain a comparable level. The idea of what constitutes luxury, it seems, is always shifting.

The reality that our notion of luxury constantly changes makes it very difficult to reengineer the process of our day-to-day work. The best we can say is whether or not the income level presently generated by our work is relatively satisfying. If it is not, then we need to choose another *way* of working, or another *field* of work, one which will produce a higher level of luxury.

This may indeed be important to some people and necessary, but I must confess to some skepticism. What we usually find, once we have made the dramatic changes necessary to achieve more wealth, is that we are no happier than before. This is not because we are not wealthier. It is because in making those changes we often damage ourselves and those around us. Reengineering for luxury usually means investing heavily in either high risk strategies (for example, making political alliances in the workplace, or trying to judge the direction of a turbulent economy) or spending family resources of health and time. And, if we are successful at gaining a new level of luxury, it just means a new standard against which to judge. The new, bigger house with the new Oldsmobile sits next to an even larger house with a Mercedes.

I recommend that any reengineering to achieve more wealth be done with great caution and the full support of your community and friends. If you are going to seek promotions, new jobs, or better financial opportunities, you need to do it in consultation with others. Get feedback on the likelihood of success, the cost involved, and the best way to proceed. Friends, family, and associates will have a good sense of how these changes will affect you and they can help you to see the risks you are taking. We are often most blind when it comes to following our desires, and it is at this point that our community can help us see more clearly.

If you *are* planning to reengineer for greater luxury, there are two basic strategies you can follow. One is to take stock of your abilities and potential, and then try to match them with the most lucrative career opportunities available. Through relentless pursuit of these opportunities, and a lot of hard work, it is often possible to create a level of personal wealth orders of magnitude greater than those you presently experience. *Finding* the opportunities is usually the harder part. But if you allow yourself a reasonable time frame (five to ten years) and you do your research well, you can usually identify fields of endeavor where your efforts will produce excellent rewards.

In making such a major career shift it is sometimes necessary to take a downward initial move in income. Shifting fields usually means starting over, and that is likely to mean a short-term reduction in pay. Entry-level corporate lawyers make less than teachers with only a few years of experience. However, the growth curve in income for a good corporate lawyer means that after only a few years he (rarely she) can pay as much in *income taxes* as a teacher with years of seniority makes to begin with. Management consulting, another potentially very lucrative field, happens to have a very high dropout rate due to the difficulty of getting established. It takes time, at very low income levels, to establish the connections, reputation and regular clientele, in order to earn a high income. The key, regardless of the career you wish to pursue, is to do your research and to work very hard.

The other strategy is to leverage your existing opportunities through promotion or by moving to a different employer within the same field. The key here is attitude. In order to be selected for

employer, you must demonstrate a determined
provement of organizational performance. The
plored for every opportunity for improvement.
ompetitors (which will serve you well if you
ther employer) and new processes can serve
, virtual university, or other training should be
ake use of every opportunity.

ategy result in a rapid quantum shift in income
level, but it is *safe* and rarely means taking a cut in pay in order to
proceed. Even if you do not succeed with your efforts, it is a rare
manager who cannot see the added value of someone who tries to
improve things. At the very least, it may mean keeping your job when
others lose theirs. While existing opportunities rarely jump you to
the head of the pack, they will help you to make steady gains.

Reengineering for Self-esteem

Far too many of us, even when we enjoy our work, take a battering
in the self-esteem department during our work day. This should come
as no surprise when we realize that the basic model used to define the
way we work is the assembly line. For a long time now, we assumed
that the more we looked and acted like mass production machines,
the better our work would be. But that assumption undercuts
everything which is genuinely valuable about us as individuals.

When we look at our work, we immediately see that our jobs are
arranged around tasks. We do *things* (like all the items on my "to do"
list). And when *tasks* become our primary focus, they soon force us to
work on their terms, not on our own. When I write a proposal for a
social service bureaucracy, I am aware that there are established
patterns and requirements I must follow if the proposal is to be deemed
acceptable. I cannot inject my personality, or have fun. Success requires

that "I" step into the background. It leaves me frustrated, and even angry. It is the technical, task driven ability to assemble the facts, figures, and program descriptions – not the personality and perspective of the person doing the work – which is deemed essential to the acceptable completion of the task. At the end of the day I come home feeling squeezed, and, as a result, sometimes inflict damage on my relationships. Sometimes my health suffers too.

The situation is common for most of us. For some of us, it is worse than what I have described. Imagine what it must be like to work on an assembly line, with all of its tedium, and to know that somewhere an engineer is trying to design a *machine* that will do your job better and faster. As we efficiently and productively go about doing our workday tasks, something vital in us gets hurt.

This has to change if we are to achieve even a minimum level of dignity in our work. We cannot go on as task-oriented persons and suffer the accompanying damage to our self-esteem. This, then, is one part of the process which must be reengineered. The question is, "How?"

I believe this aspect of our work must be changed at two levels, the personal and the corporate. Many organizations have already begun to address the problem on the corporate level through the formal management exercise of reengineering, Total Quality Management, or one of the other process-centered management restructuring tools. There have been notable successes to date in corporate redesign which have shown an understanding of processes and the human contribution to them. 3M Corporation, one of the star companies of Tom Peters and Robert Waterman's *In Search of Excellence* (Harper & Row, 1982), has made this a fact of daily life. In this highly successful company, committees, formal structures, and task dominance are substantially replaced by temporary work-groups, cross-disciplinary and cross ranks face-to-face interaction, and outcomes based activity. Day-to-day life in this company emphasizes outcomes, and front line staff work directly with vice-presidents if that is what gets the job done. Still, this exciting way of changing the nature of work is far from universally accepted.

While we must surely pay attention to this problem at the corporate level, we have just as much work to do at the personal level. We must recognize that it is up to each one of us as individuals to make the changes that will allow us to experience the meaning and self-esteem our work can generate. We must do what we can with the one thing we can change – ourselves.

LOVE

The heart of reengineering for meaning and self-esteem starts with an attitude of love. Our work must flow out of our deepest commitment to the well-being of others and of the planet. In this way we grasp the essential, and begin to find in our work, not a collection of destructive tasks, but a process where we gain and grow. When we add this attitude to our tasks, then the process becomes one of maximizing joy, and that is something which transforms tasks into good work. When we work in this way, *our transition back to home becomes one of rest and celebration.* An attitude of love is the key to making day-to-day work good work.

This is not a platitude. Very few of us work out of love. I do not mean that there is no love in us, or that it is not love that drives us. What I mean is that we have been taught that work is about tasks. Our job is to be good at using the technology and methods we have been trained in to accomplish specific goals. Love is not the key to the process for most of us. But it must be, if we do not want our work to slowly destroy us. We must love deeply those people and things we work with: our customers, our tools, our methods, our resources, and our products. Work is about transformations, and *loving transformations* are what make us whole. But loving transformations only occur when we deeply love what we are doing.

How we do this is intensely personal. I do not know how you love. You do not know how I love. All we can do is struggle to put our hearts into our work in order that our work contributes to the well-being of others as we understand it. When we do so, we feel it. We walk away from our work with intense satisfaction. Others who come into contact with our work feel it too, though they might not know what they feel or why. When our love is expressed in our work, it changes everything about our work in ways that ripple out around us.

Loving in and through our work is something we learn. I have had to learn how to stop seeing tasks and to start seeing opportunities to love. I do it by trying to see my work from an end user's point of view. If I were the one receiving this product, how would I want it to be? To quote my father, "good enough" is not good enough. I must take the extra step and test, clean up, troubleshoot, or do whatever it takes to make the product the best it can be. The words I write must be read a couple of days later, then painstakingly rewritten, perhaps more than once. Ideally, I have a good editor who then reads the manuscript, and sends it back to me for even more rewriting. And at that point, loving my work means not cursing my editor, but slowly reviewing each comment, and trying to see what it says from the *reader's* point of view. When an editor calls for clarity, I must try to revise the words to produce clarity, despite my love of the initial draft. It hurts to do so. But my love for the work must surpass my love for the sight of my own words. Good editors help in the process. They teach me how to look with a reader's eyes. I learn through the process and ideally, at the end, I have learned a little of what it means to love my work.

I hope I continue to learn. Love is not static. It means we must keep pushing ourselves into our work, trying to go further, better, faster, cleaner, and more reliably. Whatever level of excellence I have learned so far, love means pushing to find an even more excellent state. When I read, I now read not just for content, but to learn how to write. There are others much better than me at this writing business, and loving my work means seeing how they do what they do, and being humble enough to try their techniques in place of my own.

The need to inject love into our work applies just as much to those who do clerical work or assembly line work as it does to those who do "professional" work. There is not one of us who cannot put love into our work. Love can mean the difference between over-torquing or properly tightening a bolt. The worker who tightens those bolts will do his or her best to ensure that just the right stress levels are applied, so that the product performs at its very best.

Putting love into our work is not always easy. Pouring our deepest concern for others into our work leaves us exposed. Co-workers, customers, bosses, and staff can all misunderstand and mistreat us quite accidentally. If we express love through our work, we run the risk of overidentifying with it. When someone criticizes our *work*, we experience that criticism as a *personal* attack. When I give a presentation, I speak out of my experience, and with a deep concern that those in the audience gain something meaningful and practical. When they do not (and there are always those who do not) I feel devastated. I have become so involved with what I have said that I can no longer hear them and their needs.

There are other risks and benefits to this loving. I guarantee that we will suffer if we love through our work. I also guarantee that this suffering will help us become better, stronger people (though it may indicate we need to change our work or our workplace). Loving through our work transforms us into better people, but that journey of transformation is never easy. Yet although the journey is often difficult, we usually return home satisfied.

THINK POSITIVELY

This brings us to the second part of the process: thinking positively. It may seem to go without saying that if you are loving, you are positive. I only wish the two did go without saying, but it is possible to be loving and to expect that everything will go wrong.* In order to find meaning in our work and to build self-esteem, we must see the potential for positive outcomes in every situation, no matter how tough or painful it has become.

Like loving, looking for the positive is a learned ability. We have to teach ourselves that in the midst of every situation there are a number of options, at least one of which (and often many more) are positive. When we take this approach, we begin to see positive outcomes where before we saw none. Those who work with us are *also* more likely to see positive outcomes in what they are doing. When we take this approach, a certain "lightness" comes to our being and our work.

Let me be clear that I am not talking about a mindless optimism. There is nothing worse than someone who gleefully preaches that we should "be positive" when all the outcomes are stacked against us. Our positive thinking needs to be based in a realistic view of things.

I recall sitting in one gloomy business meeting. We had just been cheated in a business deal and it looked like a high-risk lawsuit

---

* My religious tradition is Mennonite, a highly conservative and socially active Protestant group, and in Mennonite thinking there is a deep connection between loving and things going wrong. Because Jesus was killed while (or because) he was doing loving work, there is an expectation that human good work, like God's good work, will likely be accompanied by much disorder and suffering.

contained the only possibility of redress. Some of us were ready to throw in the towel and take the loss. Others kept looking for a more positive resolution. Eventually, with a commitment to the positive as the *only* driving force, we worked out a deal with the other party. It was not the deal it should have been, but we eliminated most of the financial loss. The deal also kept our side involved for the long term, something which had positive possibilities attached to it.

Thinking positively is also a way of dreaming based on accomplishment. Being positive can mean (realistically) saying, "We have come so far, I am sure we can go further." This is important too, because our accomplishments can blind us to possibilities as much as our failings. There is something about human nature that loves a challenge. We need our dreams, and thinking positively is sure to create them.

BE OPEN TO TRANSCENDENCE

Finally, in order to experience meaning and self-esteem in our work we must see our work as taking place in the context of a "higher" power. We do not work alone. We work in the context of powers which fill our world with their presence, and which we can either work with or against. In some cases, I am certain that our lack of self-esteem results from fighting against or running from the godliness that lives inside each one of us. And just as much, there are times when we are struck by the overwhelming sense that we have done something profoundly right, and we have no idea why.

Once we have this awareness, our work changes – again. We start trying to "listen" to our work, to hear what it may be saying to us, about ourselves, about our task, and about the world around us. Once we understand that our work takes place in the context of those higher powers, we start trying to align our work with the vision of the world those powers inspire within us. When we start to do this, our work becomes filled with "goodness," it takes on a character of its own apart from us, and we become vessels for its unfolding.

I know of nothing more esteem building, even in the midst of difficult circumstances, than feeling that our work has become *more than our work*. We all, I believe, need to participate in *transcendence*, to contribute toward the ultimate good of the universe, and in our work it can happen. When it does, we return from work thrilled to be home, thrilled to step back from our work, and thrilled to be part of the human community at all levels.

Of course, as we reengineer our work, the tasks are still there, waiting to be done. But we may find that the tasks themselves have changed. Once we have this new set of attitudes, we often find that our judgment about what to do, or even what methods to use, have changed. One labor mediator I know talks about how consensus became a term with meaning to him, once he changed the way his work flowed from his life. Till then, he worked to see that lines were drawn and adhered to. His style was one of very tough confrontation. Now, in trying to make his work fit with the rest of his life, he has become far less confrontational and more consensual. The new approach, he says, is no less effective.

I am convinced that when we open ourselves to the realm which transcends us we begin to find new pathways and see new options. It is then that we are at our most creative, and when human creativity is positively unleashed, it knows few bounds. We can do new and better things, and there are higher powers who will work with us to discover them.

Facing Personal Renewal

I hope it is clear by this point that personal reengineering for good work is not just about changing our perspective. It is not that we have simply changed our minds and now we are happy. Reengineering involves a lot of *inner* work, the goal of which is to help us live differently in a very real way so that we can make the transition from home to work and back again as fully human and celebrating beings.

That said, it is important to recognize that this is not an easy task. There is nothing more difficult than transforming ourselves. We throw up barriers, pretend we have changed when we have not, and generally try to avoid our problems. More often than not, when we make real change it is because we have to, not because we want to.

A Vision of Personal Character

In order to make these changes, I believe we need a new vision of ourselves. Inside our heads, we have many frames of reference, images which tell us how we should behave in different circumstances. Often we deal with day-to-day life by subconsciously "flipping" through those frames until we find the ones we think apply. By changing these frames of reference, or by adding new ones, we begin to change the way we operate day to day.

When I go to work, I "flip" on my work character. I am not always *proud* of that character – tough, clear, to the point, independent, distrustful of authority, and less than happy about compromise – which I sometimes personify as a cowboy. He is capable of doing a tremendous amount of work under sometimes arduous conditions. But what he is not always good at is listening to feelings, or developing relationships with staff (customers are a very different issue). Nor is he good a dealing with human politics. (He would rather be out riding the range.) Recently, my cowboy toughness got me into a corner I could not get out of. I frightened a potential partner half to death by my willingness to walk straight into a highly complex and risky situation, confident that all would be well. The potential partner, a more cautious type, backed out. I lost a good opportunity. In retrospect, a different frame of reference, one more sensitive to feelings, would have served me better by helping me build a relationship of trust which would have enabled us both to proceed into that situation.

Nor is my personal work framework naturally open to the divine presence. It is hard for my cowboy to do much more than express the notion that God gave us brains to figure things out for ourselves. That framework does not assist me to find those places where the divine purposes and my work come together.

The Hard Work of Developing Character

I struggle to find other frames of reference that will allow me to be the loving, positive, god-centered worker I want to be. I do it by looking for images, stories, and people who represent another way of doing things. I read books and magazines looking for other ways of seeing and doing work. I look for people who speak to me of ways of working which are better than my own. I know that there are better ways of working, and I try hard to find them.

When I *do* find them, I try them on. I try to act the way I imagine the characters in a story might act if they were in my situation. Or I ask myself, "What would so-and-so do in this situation?" As I imagine how they might have acted, I begin to see new ways for me to act. This does not mean I always act the way they do. Rather, I contrast my thoughts with what their thoughts or actions might be. If the result feels okay, then I try that behavior.

One of my mentors is wonderfully direct in a way that makes you realize he cares for you. Every time I am with him I watch him, I listen to the words he chooses, the way he speaks, so that I can learn how to be more like him in my directness. Another acquaintance of mine just made a major shift out of a partnership to working on his own. He is a much gentler person than I am and so I watch to see how he makes his way through the difficulties of business on his own so that I can teach myself a gentler path through business. He also has a developed sense of the divine presence in his work and so I listen to his words about how the divine works in and through him, to give me clues to how and where I should look for the divine presence in my own work. Particular stories of business people in the news, or characters in novels, offer other glimpses of strategies I might try. All around me are people and stories which suggest alternative paths through life.

Still, I am careful about whom I try to emulate, and how I emulate them. Not every "saint" is someone I should copy. My personality is my own, and it will only bend so far. I have learned, for example, that the boisterously outgoing are not good people for me to try to be like, regardless of how wonderful they may be. I cannot do what they do, no matter how hard I try, and I only become exhausted in the attempt. I look for people who are at least somewhat like me, so that I already have something in common upon which to build.

Sometimes a mentor's approach does *not* work, and at those points I try to understand how I can do something different. One of my very wise teachers was fired from his position. It was a brutal, drawn-out event, and I watched how he responded. It taught me a lot about what to do, and what *not* to do, and I have been very clear ever since how I try to be both like and *unlike* him in my own times of difficulty. Often, I see my own strategy being reinforced. Sometimes who we are is the best we can be in that situation and change would not be a good thing.

A Continuing Journey

Reengineering to become a loving, positive, divinely sensitive worker is a long journey of many little steps. We take some of those steps voluntarily. Too many of them are forced upon us. But regardless, we progress toward sainthood.

The good news is that once we start, we rarely turn back. The rewards are too great. Our journey from home to work and back again becomes more fluid, less jarring, more supportive, and more affirming. Too many of the distinctions which trouble us are artificial, and once we start along this path they drop away and the essence of our work stands revealed. There are very few of us who, once we have tasted the esteem and worth that loving through our work can bring, will ever trade it for the old ways of wage slavery and toil. And who, having sensed the divine presence at her side, can help but continue?

6

Surfing the Workplace

———

One man I know spends his time on the way to work praying. He says he actually enjoys the rush hour. It is a time of meditation and prayer while he drives the familiar route from home to office. Once at his office, he straps on a telephone headset, and from then till he leaves work at the end of the day he is a blur of words, incoming and outgoing, as he brokers cars. He says he used to find his day stressful, but since he started praying his way to work, it has become far easier.

I spent a good part of one afternoon interviewing him at work, as the incoming calls interrupted our conversation. I had been told that he was a very spiritual person who had done a good job of bringing together his work and his faith. It certainly seemed to be true. He exuded peace, and what he had to say reflected a picture of someone who had put all the pieces together, starting at the core and working outward.

But I found that he saw the picture quite differently. For him, it was the frenzy of his work which forced him to become a more spiritual person and to get the rest of his life together. His work had been driving his life, taking more and more time, pushing aside family and friends. In response, he looked to the neglected spiritual side of his life and built a new way of working. He started doing spiritual exercises, at the beginning and end of his day, to help him keep a clear sense of the big picture. These steps had changed the way he worked at its most fundamental level. Despite being interviewed by a total stranger while handling calls in which thousands of dollars were at stake, he remained very calm. His maturity, grace and presence beamed out in the midst of the chaos.

When I think about the worker of the future, this man keeps coming back to my mind. He lives daily in the midst of the chaos of work in our world – rapidly changing, customer focused, information-based, and owner-worker driven. His workplace is more stressful than many. Yet he has found his way to peace within it, a peace driven by vision and character. And his abilities and attributes can guide the rest of us too.

Surfing

The metaphor which the car broker's style brings to my mind is that of surfing. This word has recently become associated with the Internet, but I think it is also an apt way of describing how we can live in the midst of our working chaos. Imagine a surfer hanging on a wave, a constantly changing tension of water, board, and muscle. Or think of a wind surfer balancing wind and gravity against the waves. The goal in surfing is to find that point where the body unconsciously responds to every change in wind and water. When that point is achieved, a breathless grace dances across the water. That is the way we can live in our work, from nine to five.

Think about the world in which we work. Customers come and go at a blinding pace. Companies change with mergers, buyouts, and collapse. Markets, economies, and jobs turn quickly. The dollar is down, then the dollar is up, and profits and jobs shift just as quickly. Then technology changes and everything else changes, too. Who knows what will happen next? The world of work is not a stable environment. It reminds me more of the moving waves than solid land. The best we can do is find a wave that will take us in the direction we want to go. Perhaps, in the midst of the action, we can find a *way of living* which brings vision and character together, and thereby achieve the surfer's breathless grace.

Our quest is to find those tools and techniques which will help us to "surf" our workplaces. We need to learn how to work in peace, to find peace in the midst of work, and to become aware of the sacred. Once we have found techniques that work for us, we can become more like the car broker, unshaken even by the frenzy of deal-making, for whom the boundaries between "sacred" and "secular" are gone.

Workplace Prayers

As I talk to those who move effectively through their workplace chaos, I find one thing they have in common. They all pray – pray, or meditate, or do centering exercises. Most start their working day with prayer. Some do these exercises on the way *to* work, some while *at* work, and some on the way home *from* work. The car broker spends his drive to work in meditation. An executive I know starts her day with a time for devotions. A consultant takes little breaks, just a few seconds long, throughout his day, to center himself. Each of these exercises has the same effect: it brings the "doer" back to his or her center, back to the big picture, back to the why and how of their work.

Many people associate prayer with childhood table graces, or long periods of silent meditation. They fail to see that spiritual centering can take place in the middle of the work day. But opening ourselves to the possibility of prayer at any moment can be done, and when it *is* done, it changes us profoundly. By learning new models of prayer which fit the way we live our lives, we can gain the grounding we need, when we need it.

FLASH PRAYERS

One of the techniques a mentor taught me was something he called "flash prayers." We had been discussing how to pray in the midst of day-to-day activity. It is no easy thing to pray, particularly when we think of prayer as formal, memorized words, or as requiring careful concentration. My mentor taught me to "hold" thoughts and images briefly in mind, bringing their being into my being for just a few seconds. In this way, we might learn to feel and act with respect to the sacred in that moment.

Now, when I am going into a meeting, I pause just for a moment and take a deep breath. While slowly exhaling, I turn inward and focus on my muscles, imagining what it is like for my heart to be beating at that moment. Then I take a second breath, and on the exhale I imagine the faces of those I am meeting with, or one of the people I am meeting with, and try to feel and honor their sacredness. All it takes is two or three breaths, and my relationship to those I am meeting with has changed.

Of course, the feeling this engenders is fleeting. We cannot live in this state very long. We are always caught up in what is happening around us, and we lose that attention almost immediately. But then, in the midst of the meeting, I *remember* that exercise, and it reminds me to honor my spirit, the spirit of those in the room, and the sacred presence which flows in and through each one of us.

I also notice that these flash prayers often have the very practical effect of keeping me calmer. As well, they help me to see things from the point of view of others in the room, a necessary part of creating constructive relationships. Most importantly, sometimes they help me see the way we need to work together to find the common good.

I can also use flash prayers to remind myself of the community outside of the workplace. These people, too, can be brought to mind and honored in those fleeting seconds I can find here and there during the work day. Wherever I am, in tiny moments, the sacred can emerge, if only I "flash" myself open to it.

REPETITIVE PRAYERS

Repetitive prayers are another technique some use to find the sacred in the midst of the day-to-day. Thinking up a prayer, or finding the right method of meditation for any given moment can be hard, and to make prayer easier many people repeat a brief phrase. It may be something they have written. It may be taken from a powerful poem, or a sacred scripture, or come from one of the many religious traditions. The point is to find a line, a few words, which say something important about our relationship to the essence of the universe.

In the Orthodox tradition of Christianity, the Jesus prayer uses repetition to do just that. The one praying repeats over and over the line, "God have mercy on me, a sinner." In this prayer, the Orthodox worshiper is called to affirm a basic understanding of his or her relationship to the universe, and opens him or herself to that source of spiritual energy.

By repeating this line in the midst of the day, we recall the big picture and are brought back to a grounding point. As repetition wears it into our lives, it becomes a point of reassurance, and a window into the universe as it "really" is.

There are many other such prayers; most non-Western traditions have them. Repetition has long been known as a way of moving out of the ordinary and into the spiritual, and even in the workplace this exercise can have an effect. Repetition seeks to make us aware of the essence of the sacred. It brings us out of ourselves and the transience around us, and back into the presence of our unchanging core.

The one drawback of these prayers is that they can take years to become fully effective. As the person praying slowly learns to hear, in the repeated words, the essence of the universe, and begins to change in response, the words come alive. After many years of practice, repetitive prayer can have an almost instantaneous calming and centering effect.

DEVOTIONAL PRACTICES

Devotions are structured prayers or periods of meditation which are often anchored around repetitive features in the day. One executive I know has a routine she follows every day at work. She follows a pattern of readings and prayer based on the Bible, including prayers used by the church throughout history. Every weekday morning, she reads the scripture text selected for that day and then follows with a prayer selected for the time of day and season of the year. The details change, but the daily routine is the same.

Devotional practices are much more complex than repetitive prayers, but they still function to ground the person using them. They require access to spiritual resources and often take years to develop as one piece gets added to another to form an empowering whole.

SYMBOLS

Visual images can be powerful cues as well. Most of us have some personal memento in our workplace, very often a picture of our family or life partner. Similarly, we can use symbols to remind us of what is essential to our lives. Images of saints, nature, or special symbols discreetly placed in our workplace can remind us who we really are and what we are really trying to accomplish in a larger sense. Though candles, incense, and various aromatics are inappropriate to most workplace settings, they can be helpful too. The key in each case is to find something which throws us out of our everyday consciousness and helps us remember what is important.

CENTERING EXERCISES

Centering exercises can be an ongoing part of work life, or something used in times of stress. There are any number of these exercises, but what they all have in common is "attending." Attending to the rhythm of our breathing – paying attention to *how* we inhale and exhale, and the *rate* at which we do it – is particularly common. As you do this, the tension dissolves in the rest of your body, with the effect that you are more relaxed and alert, and more sensitive to the issues confronting you.

Often, breathing or attending exercises are combined with visualization exercises. Visualization helps us fix certain thoughts or images in mind to assist in internal clarification. One visualization technique I use under times of extreme stress is to imagine myself behaving calmly and competently in the midst of my work. From that image, I can often gain a better sense of perspective, while at the same time the breathing exercise calms me inwardly. I may not become the person I wish I was, but for the moment I can take a few steps in that direction.

Workplace Community

Community is a difficult word to use these days. We do not know true community when our lives seem so transient and intimacy is difficult to find. Talking about *workplace community* is even more difficult. Our workplaces suffer because they focus on tasks, rather than our relationships. How, then, do we find in our workplaces the type of community which will help us live well?

For some this question is not important. Some of us have such a strong family, or so many good friends, that the need to find community in the workplace does not seem urgent. But for many others of us, work is one of the few places of continuity in our lives. In the midst of variety and transience, those we work with become the important constants. Particularly when our families and most important relationships are shattered by crisis, the workplace is one place we turn to for community.

As we strive to become more whole in our work, how can we build the type of community which heals and helps? Asking this question is key to finding a community of fellow travelers in our workplace, a group of people moving with us on the journey of our lives.

WORK TOGETHER

The first step is to learn to work together. This may seem obvious. For many of us, it is already so normal that we do not even think about it. We go about being supportive and friendly to those we work with, assisting others, and going out of our way to make the workplace a comfortable environment. Although not all workplaces function this way, by working together we can make even the most difficult workplaces more humane.

BE POLITE AND FRIENDLY

The attempt to build community starts with our attitude to one another. Practicing polite friendliness is a good way to begin; it goes a long way toward opening a workplace to community. A balance of politeness and friendliness can create a space in which trust and caring will grow. Having this attitude toward everyone, regardless of whether or not they deserve it, has a tremendous impact on our relationships. It makes difficult circumstances easier. It creates an environment open to communication.

Together, politeness and friendliness allow distance and approach, and a comfortable environment for others to choose a response. While politeness and friendliness may not bring us the intimacy we are looking for, they go a long way toward creating a healthy and healing workplace.

COMMUNICATE CLEARLY

Clarity in our communication is another strategy we can use to build workplace community. Most of us have heard the admonition "Let your yes mean yes, and your no mean no." Yet we all too easily forget how important it is. Being clear about what we can or cannot do, will or will not do, is essential for building trust and cooperation.

Often, our tendency is to inflate some of our capabilities, and underrate others, particularly when doing so will provide us with an advantage. We may try to meet other people's expectations, even when those expectations are out of line with reality. But we must be clear about our intentions and abilities. Only when other people find a coherence between our words and our actions will they trust our words.

Naturally, we tend to respect and want to be around those who are open about their strengths and weaknesses, and give realistic appraisals of their work. Deadlines agreed to and met can build powerful bonds between people. Quality levels agreed to and achieved create a solid working foundation. They also build trust. If what you say is accurate in one area, then I am likely to believe what you have to say in another area.

We can never overestimate the impact of clear communication on a workplace. Once someone takes the risk of being clear about their intentions, once someone demonstrates coherence between their words and their deeds, whole relationships can change. Immediately, a new standard of behavior emerges, one which encourages everyone to be more coherent, more honest, and more open. For most people, a positive pattern of communication grows, to the point where it becomes hard to resist.

I have found that this level of communication is also an excellent marketing tool. My first strategy with a potential customer is to be completely clear about what I can do, how I will do it, and when it can be done. I also inform the customer about what I will not do, and why. I do this using simple, straightforward language. Most of the time, I find that the potential customer opens up to me and becomes more honest about what they are looking for, saving both of us time and money. Sometimes I can assist the customer in deciding what they want, giving me a huge competitive advantage. Even when I do not get the contract, I have left the door open to effective future conversations.

Of course, there are two sides to this. It does not work if your attempt at honesty and clarity is met with resistance. One work group I know about tried to tell their vice president that the new database system they were working on would not be ready by its target date. But rather than working with the work group to understand, the vice president told the group that the program *would* be ready by the target, and that he would inform the president of that fact immediately. The group, despite best efforts, was nowhere close to completion when the program was announced. So they produced a small portion of their new system, calling it "Phase 1," even though it had yet to be debugged and could not function without the rest of the system. Other than the vice-president, no one was satisfied. Morale was shot, tempers frayed all around, and operators were given an unusable system.

LISTEN

This points to a fourth strategy for creating workplace community: listening. The willingness to listen plays an essential role in healing and health. Perhaps "attending" might be a better term, because listening is usually about words, and the behavior I am describing has as much to do with observing and responding as it does with hearing words.

The attempt to build healthy community involves listening to the life of the workplace, listening to what is going on behind the words of each person. When I speak, I communicate at least two different messages. The first message has to do with the *content* or the formal information I am trying to convey through my words. The second message has to do with what this content or information means to me, and is communicated in my tone of voice and body language.

Of the two messages, the second is more often neglected than the first, but it is extremely important to community. In our tone of voice, the way we stand or hold our hands, our level of muscle tension, we indicate our inner state, our relationship to the others in the conversation, the level of urgency we feel, and a thousand other things. While a person's *words* may be about work issues, the non-verbal signals may indicate hope for the future, disdain for a colleague, urgency toward a task, worry about a child, or pleasure in the view outside the window. Good community happens when we attend to the full range of communication and learn to discern and respond to its non-verbal aspects. Attending to non-verbal cues can prompt us to ask, "Is there something else?" when we detect an underlying concern.

Attending-type listening does not stop with individuals. It is also something we need to learn to do with groups. Suppose that one work group you meet with bubbles with enthusiasm all the time, while another group may be much quieter. It may be that there are two different work styles in action. Or perhaps there are problems in one of the work groups. By attending to the differences, we can pick up on details, ask questions, and learn what is really going on.

One acquaintance told me that when he took over his department he immediately noticed some sort of problem in the way the men and women were responding to each other. He could feel it, but he could not name the source of it. He could not understand what was happening until he made a trip to the women's washroom. Sexist graffiti covered the walls; some of it had been there for years. Having made that discovery, he could begin to address the issues it represented and build a better working environment.

Work groups develop their own language and patterns of communication. Habits become ingrained, and new workers soon learn the non-verbal rules of the group. These patterns can be as obvious as two groups of people refusing to talk to each other, or as subtle as using a particular unspoken way to reward creativity. Good listening means attending to all forms of communication.

SET WORK GROUP VISION

One highly powerful way of creating workplace community is to foster group vision. All of us need a sense of what our work is pushing toward. Is it to have the best customer service in the mall? Or is it about "redefining compassion," as one social service agency proclaims? We need a sense of the big picture in order to feel good about what we do.

Sometimes corporations circulate their "big picture" in a mission statement which everyone in the organization feels part of. When this is not the case, it falls on us as individual workers to proclaim such a vision. As those who care about healing and health, we need to proclaim a vision for our work. It may encompass the whole company, or just relate to our smaller area of responsibility.

Merely proclaiming such a vision is not enough. It must be demonstrated. This means telling stories about how particular work actions brought the vision to life and saying, "Well done," when someone's actions reflect the vision.

FORM ACCOUNTABILITY GROUPS

But what if the workplace itself is not conducive to community? Perhaps employees work off-site, or on different shifts. The car broker, who spends almost all of his time on the phone, uses an accountability group to build community. The accountability group is a group of people who voluntarily get together, often early in the morning, to talk, share, and find support.

In accountability groups, members pledge to be honest. They agree to be open about what they are feeling, thinking, and doing. In turn, the group agrees to support the individual, to confront him or her (gently) when the group sees a need for confrontation, and to assist each other in personal and professional growth.

Larger employers sometimes find these groups springing up among co-workers. The group the car broker is part of consists of people he has known for many years, plus a few others that the various members have more recently met. These folk get together every week or so over breakfast, to talk, share, and journey together.

Unless we allow them to, very few people outside of our families know much about us. This fact of urban life drives accountability groups. We rarely have the opportunity to react to the heart issues of a wide range of people, and therefore have little opportunity to learn from them. Refusing to make ourselves vulnerable or to allow people to see us and react to us as we really are may make life easier, but it deprives us of many opportunities for growth as persons. Accountability or support groups help us move away from the surface of our lives to see the deeper structures. Because they are not as close to us as family, they can sometimes see our lives more clearly and suggest how we might become more effective.

Diet and Exercise

One of the separations we tend to make in our lives is between diet and work. We tend to think of diet in terms of health, forgetting that health has a great deal to do with our ability to function well at work. When I interviewed the car broker, I noticed that he drank mineral water, not coffee or a soft drink. He was attending to his well-being through what he took into himself.

Many people find that as they begin to take care of themselves, certain parts of their diet naturally change. Coffee and doughnuts, dietary staples in many workplaces, are not the type of food which generate peace in the workplace. Their high chemical (coffee is a soup of complex and powerful chemicals, of which caffeine is only the most well-known), fat, and sugar content changes brain and body chemistry. Attending to the spirit is much more difficult when we stuff the body with unhealthy foods.

What we put into our bodies has a profound effect on what we produce. High fiber foods, a vegetarian or at least low-meat diet, and lots of water improve our ability to think, pray, and act. Eating more fruits and vegetables can make us more effective spiritually, and in every other way. I find yogurt to be extremely helpful for re-establishing body equilibrium. Cut back or eliminate high-fat foods, meats (especially red meat), coffee, and alcohol. Abstaining can mean social isolation in some workplaces, and it may not fit well with critical parts of work life (meals with customers, for example). In these cases, care and attention to other parts of our diet during other times of day may be adequate.

Exercise is also crucial to our physical and spiritual well-being. Our bodies need to be in reasonably good physical shape if we are to think, pray, or act well. Getting 20 minutes of physical exercise every couple of days is a good idea for everyone and going for a walk over lunch is a good way to begin. For years, I walked to and from work, a brisk 20-minute journey each way. I could not do it every day due to the weather, but most days it was not a problem. The level of well-being those walks engendered in me cannot be overestimated. I felt better, thought better, and did better work. We need to keep ourselves moving in order to function well at every level of our being.

Rest and Sleep

Much like diet, rest is an often neglected part of work life. The ancients, it appears, knew a lot about the importance of rest – things we have largely forgotten. I was amazed to find in my reading of the Bible, for example, that the subject of work is usually found in the context of rest.

In the world of the ancient Israelites, rest from work is a sign of God's blessing. In the story of the creation of the world which is told in the biblical book of Genesis, God creates the world in six days. At the end of each day, God looks at what has been created and declares it "good." At the end of the sixth day, God looks at *all* the work of the previous days and declares it "very good." Then, on the seventh day, God rests. (Genesis 1:1–2:3)

The ability to rest was a sign that the world reflected God's ideal. Not only that, rest becomes *part* of that ideal. God blesses the seventh day, the Sabbath, and declares it holy. This idea becomes so important that a later tradition even states that if only all Jews would keep the Sabbath one time, then the kingdom of God would come.

Rest speaks of the holy. We need it, if we are to become fully spiritual and whole beings.

In our machine modeled culture, this ancient wisdom has often been obscured. We describe rest the way we describe the breakdown of a machine, in terms of "down time." We tend to see the need for rest as a sign of weakness.

Rest involves taking breaks from our work. Our bodies and minds respond better to working for shorter periods of time on a variety of tasks, than for longer periods of time on a single task. We need to move from chore to chore, and stretch and rest in between. These breaks restore our judgment, assist our insight, and bring back our ability to concentrate. Taking a break from our work allows our mental energies to regroup and, when we come back, we often find that a difficult problem has solved itself.

Our attitudes to sleep are not much different than our attitudes to rest. We praise people who get by on less than eight hours of sleep, as if they were somehow more virtuous. I know of one industry consultant who delights in describing sleep – only half jokingly – as a "bourgeois affectation," and who takes great pride in the fact that he only needs four hours of sleep a night. Anyone who regularly gets eight hours of sleep may even be called "lazy."

Yet it is clear that regular sleep has an immediate impact on our ability to work. One study indicates that the effects of sleep deprivation are *cumulative* and that even tiny amounts of sleep deprivation – as little as one hour per night – immediately reduces intelligence*, and

---

*The measure used was IQ score, which showed a direct correlation of a two point drop for every hour of sleep lost. Thus, someone who sleeps in on the weekend, but who gets only seven hours of sleep Monday to Thursday, shows an eight point drop in IQ by Friday. This drop is not present in those who get a full eight hours of sleep. Those who get by on only six hours of sleep show a 16 point drop in IQ, one full standard deviation (the difference between high and normal intelligence, or between normal and learning disabled.

that high levels of sleep deprivation lead to sloppiness, impaired judgment, accident, and injury.

We need regular sleep – usually eight hours for full functioning. This often means going to bed earlier, and cutting out some non-work activity. For those who take work home with them, it may mean letting some things go undone. While this may be hard to do at first, in most cases the decrease in hours worked is more than made up for because well-rested people can work much more effectively and efficiently.

If you cannot get eight hours of sleep at night, try napping. Even short naps have a powerful rejuvenating effect.

So far, I have really only described the physiological need for and benefits of rest and sleep. But rest and sleep are important parts of spirituality as well.

Sleep brings dreams, and dreams are important to our well-being. They tell us things about ourselves and our relationships which are otherwise sometimes hard to see. Sometimes, they confirm things we already suspected.

During one stressful period in my life, I dreamed a particular pattern of dream over and over. Eventually, I began to see that the structure of the dream reflected my work. Even though the images were fantastic (flight engineer on a crash landing space shuttle), the basic pattern of the dream revealed my work situation. Indeed, at that time I was not in control of my work, but was trying hard to keep a highly destructive organization operational.

Truthfully, I do not always attend to my dreams. They often have to break through with a repeated pattern, or a particularly vivid image before I begin to puzzle over them. But I cannot ignore that in my dreams essential parts of my work may come to my attention.

Daydreams are important too. When we daydream, we allow our minds to wander down paths that mean something to us, paths which may include our work. The content of our work daydreams may tell us something about our values; we may gain a clearer vision of ourselves, or find a source of inspiration. When we daydream, we open another channel through which the spirit can speak to us.

Likewise, rest plays an important role in shaping who I am. Even though I have sometimes been called a workaholic, rest is fundamentally important to my working spirituality.

In our usual states of rush and exhaustion, patience and care can get pushed aside. But when we are well-rested, we tend to be more patient, more gentle, and more willing to live with our work and our colleagues. When we are well-rested, we have a greater capacity to attend to the details of our work. Rest allows us to *create* harmony in the workplace and to bring our work to proper completion.

There is yet another side to work which benefits from rest. The ancient Jews recognized that it is not only people who need rest, the land does too. And so sabbatical laws stipulated that every seven years, the land should lie fallow for a year. They saw the world around them as having its own life, with its own rhythms and needs. Today, in some places on the prairies, where fields have been planted and harvested year after year with little break, the soil has become damaged and erosion has become a major problem. Likewise, many of our forests are in need of rest from heavy logging, and some of our fish stocks from over fishing. Today, the world around us needs a sabbatical rest as much as it ever has.

Yet it is not just ecological systems which need the opportunity to recover equilibrium. Even in a technological and urban environment, our work needs to be attended to within its own pattern of activity and rest. Sometimes our work needs a rest from *us* as much as we need a rest from *it*. This is particularly true for managers, for activities such as planning and evaluation, and for tasks related to human development and community activity. Sometimes, our work creates a dynamic which twists relationships out of shape and we need to back off so that these relationships can regain equilibrium. Sometimes, staff perform better when managers oversee and meddle less.

Allowing ourselves to rest from our work, and our work to rest from us, is essential. At the very least, we come back to our work with fresh eyes. And sometimes, in our absence, the work reveals itself, and we come back to find something other than what we left.

We lose much when we ignore rest. We fill our working days with frenetic activity and long lists of mundane tasks, and then wonder why we are tired and the important things never seem to get done. When we rest, the truth can emerge.

7

Confronting the Darkness

—

A number of years ago I met the senior manager of a large company. He had started working for this company immediately after graduating from high school, and had earned one degree and almost completed a second in his spare time. He was well-respected, an able trouble-shooter, and was regularly called in to help divisions experiencing problems. Staff usually spoke very highly of him.

When I met him I was stunned by the contrast between the man I had heard about and the one I saw. While he was superficially charming to talk to and seemed to demonstrate competence, it seemed as if a choking cloud of depressing blackness hovered around him. Our initial conversation was twisted and confusing. He appeared at least ten years older than he was. He was also in extremely poor health, and I feared that at any moment he might collapse. It did not help that he was chain smoking and drinking his way into a stupor at the time.

I got the impression that this man was a destroyer, not a creator. The hackles on my neck tingled the whole time I was with him, and I felt "slimy" after he left. Despite his good reputation, he struck me as the most "evil" person I had ever met.

I met him again ten years later and I was amazed at the change. The black cloud was gone. While his health was still poor, he seemed in much better shape than I remembered. He was certainly clearer and more positive. While I would not call our conversation enjoyable, it did not leave me with bad feelings.

I learned, for example, that he had taken early retirement after 40 years of what he regarded as hell. He had hated his job – hated what he had to do, and hated the way the company worked. The black cloud was not him, but his job.

I also learned why he had been so effective in his job and why I had been so shocked by the contrast between his reputation and the man I met. He had internalized all the things he had hated in order to protect others. He had worked hard to ensure that *others* did not experience the company the way he did, and he was trusted for it. But that internalization cost him dearly; it was what made him the man I thought of as "evil." Without the job, the evil dropped away.

The Workplace Is Never Neutral

Our work is never neutral. It either helps us become better people, and the world become a better place, or it makes us and the world worse. Regardless of the intentions we bring to it, or the position we have, our work shapes us and the world around us in very powerful ways.

When our work becomes destructive of ourselves, of our colleagues, or of our environment, we need to address the factors that make it so. The senior manager referred to above addressed the negative factors in the workplace, but in a way that was as destructive as the factors themselves. He abused his health, punished his family, and wasted a huge portion of his life in a bottle – all in an attempt to deal with the demands of his work. When he finally made the *important* change, that of leaving the job, his whole being changed for the better. I can only wonder what would have happened had he left the job years earlier. What could he have achieved in a more positive environment? His story is tragic because he could have chosen another path.

Naming the Darkness

The first step in addressing the destructive side – or the dark side or shadow side – of our work is to name it. Naming reduces the power of the shadow side over us, and gives us the power to change it. Naming enables us to identify the problem so we might see what type of change is appropriate. Naming connects us to what others have experienced and done, and shows us the place of our problem in the context of the human community. It keeps us from running from the problem, or participating in activities which make the problem worse. Naming a problem is really half the solution.

The challenge is to name things accurately. Improper naming leads to misdirected actions and to "solutions" which are not solutions at all. One highway authority decided to crackdown on speeders, having decided that there were far too many people driving above the posted limit on a particular section of highway. This raised quite an outcry. To the surprise of many, the highway authority then reviewed the situation and decided that in this case, the problem was not too many people speeding, but a speed limit which was too low. They had originally misnamed the problem and, under review, determined that people could drive considerably faster, without risk, on the identified section of highway. The speed limit was raised, with few negative consequences.

Misnaming of problems happens all too often in the workplace, particularly when it comes to personnel issues. A former employee of mine told me, after we had worked together for some time, that she had been fired from her previous job. Management had named her as the problem in the office. Her "crime" had been a bad attitude, and they had decided that the solution was to remove her. This surprised me, because I knew her as a positive, cheerful, and diligent staff member. While I cannot be sure, since I was not involved in the situation, I suspect that management had misnamed the problem, and had, in the process, let go of one of their best staff (she was, as I say, one of the pillars of our department).

Large bureaucracies are especially noted for this sort of thing. An engineer in a large company discovered one day that a number of major customers were routinely overpaying their energy bills due to a problem in the type of meter the company was using. Under a specific set of circumstances, the meter consistently read the usage at a higher than actual rate. It took him two years to have the problem recognized by senior management, and he was nearly fired in the process. His division manager, refusing to accept that the meter was the problem, was inclined to believe that the *engineer* was the problem. Word eventually got out, however, and the meters were replaced. (Management also balked at reimbursing its customers for the overpayment.)

Some problems, of course, are genuinely confusing. We can face situations where there are so many issues involved that accurate naming becomes next to impossible. Once, I bravely attacked a complex problem in church life, only to decide a year later that it was virtually "unsolvable." There were so many factors in play – matters of geography, finances, ethnicity, building structure, and tradition – that I was never sure I had really named the problem.

It is imperative, when we look at the destructive aspects of our work, that we do our best to name the root problems. This is *really* what accurate naming is all about.

Character Problems (Lying, Cheating, Stealing)

One of the problems we all face at work is dealing with those who do not treat us properly or act appropriately. No matter how isolated we may be in our job, most of us have had some experience with people who lie, cheat, steal or who are otherwise abusive. These experiences are discouraging at best and personally devastating at worst. If it were easy to identify these folk beforehand, perhaps they would be easier to deal with. But they are not easy to identify. Anyone can become a "problem" person in this regard, ourselves included.

While most of us treat each other reasonably well, all of us, from time to time, break the most basic rules of human conduct. Most of us do it out of hurt, stress, exhaustion, or illness. Our marriage is in trouble so our tempers flare and we end up yelling at a store clerk. Or we conclude that the management at work has taken advantage of us and so we feel justified in walking off with a couple of hundred dollars of equipment. At times, our judgment is impaired and we do things which we later genuinely regret. (These lapses of judgment are experienced quite differently by those on the receiving end. To them, our actions come across as abuse, violence, and misuse.)

Our best personal response can be to commit ourselves to integrity and honesty. While this may not stop us from breaking the rules from time to time, it will give us the strength to apologize and correct our behavior. Otherwise, one lapse can lead to another and slowly we, and those around us, lose our civility.

Unfortunately, the general public seems to have decided that there are some contexts in which misuse and abuse are *acceptable*. An ex-civil servant once confided to me his reasons for leaving government. He said, "You know how civil servants get a beaten-down look? It is because people beat on us. I don't know what it is, but people think that because we work for the government they can abuse us. Being out of the service is wonderful. People say 'please' and 'thank you,' and they mean it!"

Then there are those people who violate the rules of trust and honesty on a regular basis. A favorite scam in our community is to show up at a business with a load of new photocopier toner cartridges. The cartridges are delivered and the bill presented. Usually, the bill is paid long before anyone is aware that the cartridges were not ordered. Sometimes *no one* ever discovers the fraud, and the unordered and highly-priced toner just becomes part of the stock. Sometimes the fraud is only discovered after someone tries the cartridge in the machine and finds that the machine no longer works properly due to toner incompatibility – a problem which can be very expensive to repair.

These problems are not easily addressed. Both the systematically-abused civil servant and the fraud artist are caught in self-perpetuating systems. The difference is that the civil servant's situation is external, while the thief's situation is internal. Neither can be dealt with without major effort and support from a community. In these cases it may be best simply to walk away as cleanly as possible.

Addictions/Emotional Issues

Still more difficult to deal with are the destructive personal problems. There are drug addicts, alcoholics, sex addicts, and people with serious personality disorders in the workplace. Each may have a serious destructive impact on the work environment. Typically, these people are abusive at the same time as they draw people into their needs and problems. They generally, though not always, do poor work, have high rates of absenteeism, and can be extremely difficult to deal with. Sometimes they are the boss. Sometimes they are a key customer. Sometimes they are a colleague. Whoever they may be, few of us manage to avoid them altogether.

What makes these people hard to deal with is the way they manipulate those around them. Many people with serious problems are able to do just well enough to hang onto their jobs. They draw people around them who will cover up for their mistakes, assist them to meet deadlines, and feed them the emotional support they want. When confronted, they usually try to create a highly-charged emotional environment. They become swirling vortexes, casting wider and wider circles of negative energy. In many cases, the drain becomes so immense that their supporters start to break down, or become dependent (co-dependent) upon the addict themselves.

Of course, it is natural for us to want to help. Yet if we get caught up in caring for these deeply troubled people, we are headed for trouble ourselves. They will demand more and more of us, until we have nothing left to give. While most of us (hopefully) are mature enough to take responsibility for our own actions, many of these people are not. They will do anything, including destroy those who care for them, in order to avoid taking responsibility for their own behavior.

Dealing with this type of a situation when it involves a colleague, or worse yet, a boss, is extremely difficult. It seems we either end up unintentionally *supporting* the manipulator, or in *conflict* with the person or members of their circle.

The best strategy is to maintain your focus. Be very clear about your work and what you are trying to achieve. Do your best to be completely professional, clear about your communication, and polite to those around you. When confronted with a demand for support, focus your energy on doing your work and, if possible, remain detached from the problem person. Typically this will draw a hostile response, because anyone who does not prop up the problem person is seen as a threat by those drawn into the addicted circle. But holding firm is the only long-term solution. It will also allow you and energize you to continue getting your work done.

If possible, bring the problem situation to the attention of those who can do something about it. It may be wise to document behaviors, particularly if those behaviors make it difficult to do your work. The key is to focus on productivity related issues, and to do so as unemotionally as possible, since the problem person will undoubtedly try to pump up the emotional volume of the situation once confronted.

In all this beware. Unless senior management is experienced with this type of situation, their first response may be to try to pretend it is not happening; these situations consume great amounts of energy, and many managers hold to the "ignore it and it will go away" school. Also, if senior staff or management is involved in propping up the problem person, *you* may very quickly become named as the problem.

Regardless, get outside support. Have someone, or a group, to talk to. A professional counselor is a good idea. An outside support group will help you keep clear about your own issues, and provide support if the situation turns hostile.

It is wise in these situations to recognize our own limitations. Yes, we want to help. But people with addictions and personality problems need caring and firm confrontation from people who know what they are doing. We, as co-workers and associates, are rarely trained and experienced in this type of intervention. We need to stand clear and leave the major work of healing to the professionals.

In this regard, a good employee assistance program (EAP) will have resource people with experience in these matters who can help.

Unfortunately, these programs are usually only found in larger organizations. Still, smaller companies will sometimes purchase this assistance, particularly if the identified problem involves a senior staff or management person.

Termination

One of the darkest parts of work is losing it – especially through layoff or firing. And the bad news (as if termination was not bad enough) is that given the changing shape of the North American economy this experience is becoming increasingly common. Most of us will face a permanent layoff at some time in our working lives. Many of us will face it more than once. We all need to learn to accept this, to work through it, and to help others in the same situation.

Almost always, termination is not a nice process. It hurts, and always there are emotional loose ends. As already mentioned in chapter two, one of the first things to suffer is our sense of identity as workers. To add insult to injury, very often we feel we have been unjustly or unfairly treated, particularly so if we also feel we have been made a scapegoat for larger problems. Leaving may mean saying goodbye to colleagues we have worked with for years, people we have come to know as friends. If the termination was preceded by a period of conflict, these goodbyes can be strained and awkward.

Sometimes there is barely even *time* to say goodbye. Many large institutions have instituted policies which require employees to vacate the premises almost immediately upon notification of termination. Employees are required to hand over their keys and are escorted to the front door, sometimes by security guards. The lack of trust these policies reflect can be particularly hurtful to long-time workers, who have invested years in a job and who genuinely care about the well-being of the institution. Naming these as destructive practices may be a first step in finding more humane ways to go about this business, which is already destructive enough.

On the other side of things, closure can *also* be difficult for those who remain behind in the workplace. These people may have differing views on the appropriateness of the termination, and while it might help them to talk about the details, this is not always possible. Depending on the circumstances, there is often the question, "Am I next?" Managers responsible for terminations often go through agonizing self-examination, feel guilty, and themselves become less able to function. Even though, sometimes, termination is the best thing that can be done for the company and the person, it has deep and lasting effects on everyone.

For those of us who have lost our work, termination is the start of a long process of grief. We experience all the typical stages of mourning – denial and anger, bargaining and depression – until we finally come to acceptance of the loss. Then we face the roller coaster of hope and rejection while looking for new work opportunities. It can be a long, and very tough business moving from one job to another.

In making this transition it is important not to be consumed by anger or to give way to despair. These are very real emotions that anyone losing a job will go through. But as we move through this phase we must accept the feelings and not give in to seeing them as permanent. Anger and depression are valid, but if they are not balanced by a search for new opportunities and an openness to what can be learned through the experience, these emotions can quickly get the best of us.

While this next piece of wisdom may seem trite or difficult to accept by those who are still angry or are otherwise still in the emotional throws of adjustment, it is true nonetheless. Being laid off or fired is not always a bad thing. Many people look upon it as one of the best things that ever happened to them. Being laid off or fired can be a needed and positive release from a destructive job. This does not mean, of course, that these workers felt this relief immediately after losing the work. Usually, they used their down time to reevaluate their lives, assess their goals, and set a new direction more in keeping with their core identity and values. It became a positive experience because they used it to create a life which was more in keeping with their soul.

Still, I wish I could give some magic advice that would provide an easy way to get through these times, but I do not know of any. I *do* know that attitude makes a tremendous difference. My mantra in such circumstances is, "Everything will be all right." Then I reflect on my good health, the good experiences I have had, the things my work has taught me that I value and that I want to build upon. I try to recognize that no matter what I have been through, I am still a valuable and positive person.

I have found talking to others extremely valuable. I have talked to friends, neighbors, and loved ones, as often as they have let me and as long as they have been willing to listen – sometimes a little more. I have talked until I have become sick of the story myself. (At times like these it helps to have a wide circle of friends.) Always, their feedback and support has helped me keep my perspective, has given me positive reinforcement, and has served to lessen the pain. Sometimes it has also provided good leads on new work.

In short, losing our work is painful and traumatic. Sometimes it can also be transformative and life giving. Either way, our friends can help us through. And someday, we may be called upon to return the favor.

Process Problems

At first glance it may seem strange that I include process problems in a chapter on darkness in the workplace. We usually describe processes as either efficient or inefficient, whereas allusions to "darkness" seem to hint at immoral or unethical deeds.

I have included a brief discussion of processes because when I talk about darkness in the workplace, or the shadow side of work, I am really talking about anything that has a negative effect on the individual, on the work environment, on the end product, on the end user, or on our larger non-working environment. Processes may be "merely inefficient," but when they are so, they can have a negative influence on any or all of these things.

On the personal level, inefficient processes drain physical, emotional, and spiritual resources. People suffer from overwork as they waste time, energy, and resources on tasks which could be done more efficiently or effectively. This personal frustration soon sours the working environment as people start to get angry with themselves, with each other, and with the organization.

Inefficiencies in process can also negatively affect the quality of the product, and they are a common complaint of customers. One international volunteer organization I worked for typically took one to two years to process a prospective volunteer's application, although applications could at times be processed in six months. Sometimes the application process was never completed. Often, volunteers would give up and go elsewhere, particularly when they found that rival organizations could complete the same application in a matter of weeks.

Most of us, I am sure, have experienced the frustration of trying to change the mailing address of a magazine or other subscription and of discovering it can take many attempts and several months to do so.

When customer frustrations grow to significant proportions, they can threaten the very viability of the organization.

Any organization can provide better service and make more effective use of worker time and energy. It just takes some *work* and a recognition that it is the *process* that is usually the problem, not the *people*. Processes and procedures tend to evolve over time in response to changing environments and problems, almost as if they had a life of their own. Systems and procedures grow, bit by bit, as little pieces get added onto already existing structures, until one day we discover that what used to work two years ago has, in the meantime, grown enormously complex and unwieldy.

The *work*, alluded to above, involves reengineering or redesigning the process. Whole books have been written about this subject alone and I can hardly even touch on the surface of the topic. Suffice it to say that it is helpful, according to reengineering guru Michael Hammer, to outline "inputs" on one page, "outputs" on a second page, and to put a blank sheet of paper in between. Rethink everything between input and output, focusing on what needs to be done in order to ensure that the core outputs, or the primary goals, are achieved.

When reviewing processes, remember that we feel better when we work well. Each one of us has a very deep need to be productive, and wasted effort runs counter to that need.

Another concern, when it comes to process, is the issue of *access* or *participation*. Who has access to the decision-making process? Who gets to participate in the discussion when important decisions are being made?

In the past, it has not been uncommon for government, for example, to institute policies regarding land use or resource management without much consultation with or input from the communities most directly affected by those decisions. Closer to home, it is worth looking at how important decisions get made in our own places of work.

Invariably, whenever this topic is raised, arguments arise over the relative efficiencies of a top-down approach to management and decision making versus a more consultative or cooperative approach. The issues are complex and I do not want to pretend there is only one correct or easy answer.

By naming lack of participation in decision-making processes as something "dark" I simply wish to recognize the negative energies that are created when people are excluded from having input into important decisions which affect their work and their lives. The more dictatorial the work environment, the more workers feel powerless and hopeless. These feelings can quickly lead to a nonproductive apathy and depression, or an actively destructive anger and resentment.

Good work requires positive energy and attitudes. One way to create those things, I believe, is by actively encouraging as much worker participation in decision-making processes as possible.

Moral Systems

Ethics are a problem, and not because there is not "enough" ethics in the business world. We live in a world of conflicting ethical systems, where deeply held beliefs about right and wrong clash.

I hesitate to raise this issue because of its sheer complexity. Professional ethicists themselves do not agree on the nature or source of the ethical problems we face in the workplace. Yet this is another one of the areas where our work can become very painful for ourselves and for those we work with. While I do not claim to have mastered the issues, I *do* believe that we need to have a basic grasp of what they are and how we might respond. I believe this is particularly important as our workplaces begin to straddle the globe and we encounter a greater diversity of people and moral and ethical systems.

To give just a little taste of the difficulty these issues raise, ethics and morality change. For example, in North America we have learned that "humanocentric" ethics and morality are not adequate. We have learned that it is *not right* to cut down all the trees, leave gaping wounds in the Earth, or to pump poisons into rivers by the ton in order to serve *human* desires. We now believe that these activities are *wrong*. But our ecologically sensitive ethics are something new. We *once* thought that it was our *right* to do these things, that these were reasonable activities conducted by moral and ethical human beings.

But while we now know that our destruction of the Earth is not moral, we are still deeply divided when it comes to issues such as the morality of war, capital punishment, euthanasia, abortion, or any number of other issues. And it is quite possible for genuinely moral and ethical people to stand on opposing sides of the debate.

These issues, and others as well, turn up in our work all the time. Is it moral to supply parts for weapons manufacture? Is it moral to have your product made overseas when it is uneconomical to have it made at home? What if the overseas producer uses child labor? Is it moral to prescribe drugs knowing they will be used to end a life? Is it moral to operate an abortion clinic? Is it moral to be any link in the long economic chain attached to any of the above activies – to be the trucker, cleaner, accountant, or lawyer that supports the operation of these activities? Is it moral to have your product, even though passed through wholesalers and suppliers, used in any of these contexts?

There are those who answer "yes" and those who answer "no" to each of these questions. What happens if it is our boss who answers "yes" and we who answer "no"?

We have only begun to touch on the complexity, and to sense the immediacy, of these questions.

What happens when we take our "commonly held" North American ethical systems into other countries? For example, what happens when the deeply held North American belief (backed by North American law) that our families should not prosper at the expense of our business partners meets the deeply held African belief (backed by thousands of years of cultural and economic practice) that family needs precede all other loyalties? Or what about when our requirement of private ownership (the basis of our economic system) meets a Marxist commitment to collective well-being? We are not talking about abstractions. These are realities faced by companies and organizations all over the planet. Value systems – and along with them, morality, ethics, and law – clash on a regular basis.

The results range from amusing to devastating.

So what can we do? I am not sure what the answer is, or even if there is one. As I said, even professional ethicists disagree about these issues.

My personal solution is three stepped.

1. TOLERANCE

I cannot make others believe what I believe, or behave in ways I believe are moral and ethical. I *can*, however, try to be tolerant of the range of perspectives and practices of other people. Diversity is good. It is a sign of life and growth. Tolerating diversity is one way I can be open to the richness of what life has to offer, and it provides an opportunity to learn new ways of thinking and to gain new perspectives.

In chapter three I said the process of work begins with imagination. Imagination springs from, among other things, diversity. Diversity pushes us to see new needs, learn new methods, and experience alternative outcomes. New ideas and new jobs are common outcomes of the experience of diversity.

But sometimes diversity is not comfortable. As I said in chapter two, we have a need to see our own face, our own image, reflected in the world around us. Diversity can rub up against the edges of our personal comfort zone and leave us wishing that other people and processes were more like us. Many organizations and companies recognize this and have formal programs which help people to become more comfortable with diversity.

2. CLARITY

Of course, it doesn't always feel like just a matter of legitimate diversity. Sometimes the issues strike us as being blatantly *right* or *wrong*. To talk of tolerance in these situations is not very helpful. These clashes seem "either/or."

When faced with this type of situation, we should try to be *clear* about *who we are* and *what we believe.* Rarely in these ethical clashes is it a situation of good people versus bad people (no matter how much either side may wish to put it in these terms). If possible, we can try to express our ethics in terms comfortable to the other party. Clear communication breaks down barriers and can help to create a situation of *compromise.*

But few of us are that capable and articulate. Generally, the most we can say is: "Work with me. Let us walk together, and at some point in the future you may trust me regardless of how different I sound."

Herein lies one of work's greatest powers and rewards. In these situations, bridges are usually built, not out of understanding and shared language, but out of shared experience. As we work together, we learn that constructive experiences can happen for both sides. Because work forces us to join together to accomplish shared ends, it teaches us that we need each other despite our differences. We can learn to respect each other and to compromise in many places, even when we disagree profoundly.

3. RESISTANCE

Occasionally, these two strategies are not enough. As we will see in chapter nine, there are very different ways of understanding the true nature of the universe, ways of understanding which change the way we see right and wrong. Some ways of understanding the true nature of the universe may, under some circumstances, lead to *violence* against other people or the planet. At these points, I believe we are called to *resistance.*

Resistance means, first, not giving way to complicity. It means saying, "If that is what it means to be part of this, then I will not participate." Our resistance begins by disconnecting ourselves from the behavior we find immoral, unethical, or illegal.

This kind of resistance is often enough to inspire change; it is our complicity which allows behaviors we disapprove of to continue. Most people are concerned with the appearance of their actions, and when we take a stand they will often change their behavior. They may not agree with our stance, but they seek to maintain our good will and relationship. Even if this scenario seems only to postpone further conflict, that postponement may provide the necessary time for education to take place, or for a joint search for a mutually acceptable process or outcome to happen.

Unfortunately, in the workplace, refusing to participate in behavior we find immoral, unethical, or illegal, may mean we have to quit our job. In fact, quitting may be *all* we can do.

Sometimes we may need to take a *second* step of resistance, which is to say, "I will do my best to ensure that you may not continue." "Whistle-blowing" by turning to the law or to the public is one way to do this. *Boycotts* and *public awareness* campaigns can also work to change the behavior of those who will not listen. These strategies can be risky and need to happen with the support of a community.

One of the benefits of living in a *democracy* is that if we can convince a majority of people that a certain behavior is wrong, we can sometimes get government to respond and to make laws against it. While democratic action is a slow and cumbersome process, I believe it works reasonably well.

Is it ever right to resist violently? I *personally* do not believe that it is right to use violence against others, even when that violence may stop an injustice. Fortunately, this question rarely comes up in the workplace. In those few cases where it might, I recommend a long process of consultation.

Tedium

One of the basic problems we all deal with in our work, at some time, is tedium. Our tasks become wearisome and boring. Our work does not *give* us energy, but rather *drains* our energy. In some cases, this can even bring us into physical danger as our boredom causes us to lose awareness of the risks in our physical environment.

Which tasks we find draining depends very much on who we are. While I may find a particular set of routines tedious, that does not mean that others will find them so. The challenge for us here is to judge our own limits and to find ways of working within them. Personally, I hate filing. But I have learned to coexist with it in a rather messy relationship. My filing cabinet is half-empty, while files in various states of disarray are stacked on the floor, on shelves on the wall, and in bins under my desk. I do not lose things, but I *have* had to root through my recycling bin from time to time to find work in progress. When the mess gets bad enough, I sit down with a cup of tea and patiently label and put things away.

It works for me, but it certainly would not have for one of my colleagues who was of the "keep your desktop clear" school. Every day, at the end of the day, he put everything neatly away.

Filing is an *inconvenience* for me. But tedium can also be *dangerous*. When I worked in a warehouse, the tedium of waiting for another truck to arrive, or for the front desk to send an order to fill from the stacks, left me drowsy. I spent hours rearranging boxes and looking for little bits of dust in an effort to keep awake. I became sloppy in my work. Once, due to my inattention, I accidentally caused an eight-foot stack of 60 lb. boxes to topple. I was not hurt, but the experience shook me up and taught me how serious my inattention could become. What if the stack had come down on me? What if it had been a 16 foot stack? I needed to get out of that job.

How we cope with tedium is largely up to us. Sometimes a little discipline will take care of it. Other times we may need to make major changes. Either way, before we can do anything about it, we must name it.

Destructive Byproducts and Side Effects of Our Work

No matter what we do, there are destructive byproducts and side effects to our work. Waste, pollution, or product misuse all "shadow" our work. While we can never eliminate these byproducts and side effects, we need to make a commitment to respect our planet and each other. We all bear the responsibility to do the best we can with the knowledge and methods at our disposal.

We also need to seek ways of doing better. When a new approach comes along, we must be the first to risk trying it.

But reducing or ending destructive or wasteful practices is not always easy. What happens when there is no better way, or when a better way exists but implementing it is beyond our capability? At that point, we need to reach out to others in our organization and beyond in a search for assistance. Generally, it is advisable to go to people in the company first. If we are to have any hope of implementing a solution, it will only be with the support of others in the organization.

Whether or not we choose to look outside the organization for help depends a lot on the ethos of the management of the company and how sympathetic they are to the concern that has been raised. If they are sympathetic, they will probably institute a search for solutions themselves and be quite happy to accept them wherever they come from.

If they are not sympathetic, the decision to look outside for solutions becomes much more risky. Companies in this situation often find it easier to eliminate the one trying to solve the problem than to face the problem itself.

Recognizing Our Own Darkness

It is important to recognize our own participation in all forms of darkness. Each one of us brings a mixture of good and bad, helpful and unhelpful qualities to our work. Work can do bad things to us (and to the world), but we can also do bad things to our work.

It is not uncommon, for example, to take the turmoil and struggle of our personal lives and project it onto our work and co-workers. I once had a terrible relationship with a co-worker. Things went from bad to worse. Eventually I began to see my own part in what made our relationship awful. We were out on a call together and, as I glanced at her, I caught in her profile a similarity to my mother. Suddenly it hit me; I was projecting onto her some of my feelings toward my mother, with whom I was fighting at the time. That realization helped me to calm down in our relationship, and to do my part to improve things.

I would like to say that was all it took, but that was not the end of the story. She did not suddenly start treating me well just because I stopped projecting my anger with my mother onto her. Eventually I discovered that she was doing much the same thing to me. Her husband, with whom she was having a period of marital instability, bore a similarity to me. Unfortunately, we never resolved our difficulties, in part because we were also very different in other ways; we each had a different style of work, and a different sense of humor and honor.

The point is that we bring whatever is inside us – from personality issues, to health concerns, to economic fears, to ethnic history – to our work and we experience our work through those things. The darkness we experience can be a darkness of our own making. We can end up remaking our work, our co-workers, and even whole organizations in our own dark image.

I once knew a woman who saw conspiracies piled upon conspiracies. Knowing what I did about the organization, I saw some truth in what she said. But as time passed I noticed a greater discrepancy between what she said and what I observed. Especially as things in the organization changed for the better, and there was no change in the level of conspiracy she saw, I began to see that conspiracy was an important feature of her worldview. As I got to know her better, I found out that she saw conspiracies *everywhere*, not just at work.

While we do not all see conspiracies as this woman did, what was happening as she viewed her workplace was not at all unique. We all tend to have special areas of concern, things that strike us as dark and about which we may become hyper vigilant. Sometimes in our efforts to guard against those things, we lose our ability to distinguish between genuinely encroaching shadows and those we project.

Ironically, our desire *not* to see any darkness in the workplace can be just as pervasive and just as distorting. Just as we can mistake the nature of the darkness because of our own inner shadows, we can miss the darkness completely. It seems to be one of those perverse truths that we either see things as much darker than they really are, or as much lighter. The latter is particularly true when we have invested much of ourselves in our work. The founders of a company can be the last to see the signs of impending bankruptcy. The administrators of a government agency which has invested 30 million dollars in a social service program that does more harm than good can be the most reluctant to pull the plug. When we have put a lot into something, we want it to be good – sometimes to the point that we blind ourselves to the bad.

Responding Effectively

Whichever shadows we face in our work, it is important to remember that each of us is different and that the decisions we make about which shadows to challenge and how to challenge them are highly individual. We are not called to shine light into every corner of darkness or upon every lurking shadow. We can only do so much, and so we must carefully choose the places and times where we will confront the shadows. Failure to set limits will lead to its own shadowed spiral into despair and emptiness. Our challenge is to find those areas where we can make a real difference.

Of course, all of us will face certain obstacles, whether we seek them out or not. As we learn and grow, life itself will put challenges in front of us. At those times, we must do what we can with the abilities and wisdom we have available to us. Sometimes we will fail and sometimes we will succeed. Always we will grow and become wiser.

We also need to support others who are confronting their own shadows, who are taking on their own challenges. Just because a shadow is not mine to confront does not mean I have no responsibility in relation to it. I must support others by listening, acting when called upon, and generally encouraging their efforts. This does not mean we need to be at their side all the time. Tasks vary and shared perception is not the same as shared obligation. But an attitude of support will go a long way toward empowering others.

Prayer

Those who are more skeptical may dismiss this, but prayer is an effective way to challenge the shadows. I do not mean primarily the meditation that opens us up to inner reserves of strength and integrity, although this kind of prayer is effective too – and necessary. The kind of prayer I am talking about here addresses the source of the universe in lament and hope. It seeks to touch the hidden fabric behind the physical world, a fabric responsive to our touch.

In prayer, we have the opportunity to bring the darkness into the cosmic light, to expose its impact on us, and to call for change in response. As we name and raise the shadows we face into the light of the universe itself, those shadows lose some of their fundamental power.

Shadows belong to the realm of the spirit, and it is in the realm of the spirit that they need to be addressed. Obviously, we still need to take them on in the practical world of day-to-day concerns. But if we fail to address them as the spiritual issues they are, they will reappear. To put it in slightly different terms, the shadows we face in day-to-day life are *symptoms* of fundamental, spiritual problems that need fundamental, spiritual solutions. Prayer is not the definitive spiritual solution, but it is a step in the right direction. In petitionary prayer we teach the universe our needs.

While we may bring a problem to light, and while we may have a solution in mind, we have no way of knowing how the power behind the universe will respond. At that point, we live in hope. Mystery enfolds the ways of the universe and with prayer there is not always a visible or logical chain of cause and effect. Sometimes change comes in a day. Sometimes we can only detect it over generations, if at all. Regardless, I know that prayer makes a difference.

Integrity

The key to our activities is integrity. Integrity refers to a oneness of purpose, character, and intent which acts as the backbone for all our activities. If we lack integrity, our actions become shadow creators, the source of problems for others. But if we *have* integrity, our actions create light regardless of their success. When we seek to be of one mind, one will, one action, and do our best to reflect in our lives the heart of the universe, we create light. Our own integrity then calls out to the integrity in others, providing an example and creating community.

Integrity is the foundation of all effective response to shadows. When I face a crisis situation, an addict in need, or a process gone bad, my integrity keeps me pointed in the right direction. My integrity tells me I have a purpose, and that purpose is to see good come from the situation. As long as I hang onto that integrity, that purpose, I will have something to come back to as the contingencies of events and the vagaries of circumstance push me this way and that. When an addict pulls me into their world, wanting me to prop them up, my integrity calls me to account, and reminds me of another path. When I face a destructive practice, my integrity tells me that I must respond, even though it may well be easier to close my eyes.

As I act with integrity, my integrity is strengthened. It is built up over years, ingrained in *habit*, worn into the patterns of my personality. I learn to see and feel when I am living by it and when I am straying from it. As I struggle to maintain my integrity, each experience teaches me the places where I am vulnerable and the places where I am strong. I learn to seek out the places where I can be strong and build up the places I am weak.

Finally, at the end of life, integrity is one of the few things we take with us. It can be extremely tempting to shift ground, to adopt someone else's view, or to go along with the shadows. Fear for our jobs, fear of alienating friends, financial need, and exhaustion can all have us looking the other way and saying, "So what." But while we can betray ourselves in the short term, in the long term we are left wondering what we have stood for and whether there was good in our lives. At the end of the day, we walk away not with friends, possessions, or family, but with what we know about ourselves and about our God.

8

Being Whole

In the space of a few days I had separate conversations with an employment professional and a mental health professional. Both explained to me, with the bright light of fresh insight in their eyes, how they had come to see the relationship between work and the rest of life. The first explained how he now knew that a worker's mental health had a profound impact on their ability to function in the workplace. The other told me how it had finally become obvious to him that the ability of a person to do meaningful work made a real impact on their mental health. I was struck by the genuine amazement of these two people. Our work and the rest of our lives are inextricably connected, but these experienced professionals had only recently come to see it. These incidents indicated to me just how far apart our work and the rest of our lives are for most of us.

The forced separation of work and the rest of life are ingrained in our culture. But in fact, we can only do one when we are at peace with the other. We are only able to live when we know how to work and we are only able to work when we know how to live.

The Paradoxes of Life

When we try to look at our life and our work as two parts of one whole, we are immediately struck by some paradoxes.

The first paradox stems from the fact that the two really *are* different. *The rules of the workplace are not the rules of home, nor can they be. Yet we must be the same person in both places, or we find ourselves torn in two, and one or both are going to suffer.*

The tension contained in the first statement – that the rules of home are not the rules of the workplace – has led to a demand by some employers that we box our lives into separate spheres, acting as one person at work and another person as home. And yet, as the second statement points out, if we do so, something breaks and we become less than we can be, or other than we should be. Somehow, we must bridge the unbridgeable.

Part of the answer has already been suggested in chapter four, where we looked at how to shape a career that fits who we are. As we pursue a career path in keeping with our nature and values, we find much of the incompatibility between work and the rest of our lives falling away. When our work and our home life both reflect our most important values, they fit together more comfortably.

Yet even when we work in ways which reflect our most important values, plenty of opportunities still exist for home and work to clash. It is not polite, for example, to engage in some work activities outside of work; the psychologist who tries to analyze friends and family is asking for trouble. So too, the standards we demand in the workplace may not be appropriate after hours. Too much tidy efficiency at home can leave our families feeling trapped.

And so another part of the answer involves something I call "multi-tracking," finding ways to honor our integrity, while at the same time allowing ourselves to live differently in the different areas of our lives.

Protecting our relationships is a particular focus of multi-tracking. Friends and family will rarely tolerate the type of relationships which our work demands. Our goal, therefore, should be to ensure that *all* our relationships, whether at home or at work, reflect our fundamental concerns, while at the same time we allow those relationships to reflect the particular needs of either collegiality or friendship or family.

I will not, for example, treat either those at work or those at home merely in terms of their use to me (an action which would violate my fundamental concern for human value). At the same time, I will respect the fact that my work relationships and home relationships will be different. I will not necessarily try to make those at work my friends. If friendship develops, that is fine, but I will not try to enforce an inappropriate standard of friendship.

The failure to effectively draw the line between work and home is one of the major reasons we lose our equilibrium. Entrepreneurs, managers, artists, and those in the helping professions are all prone to this failure. When our work is relationship-focused or calls for all the creativity and enthusiasm we can muster, it becomes very easy to get "caught" in our work to the point that it distorts the rest of our lives: the businessman requires his children to be on display for the clients he brings home on the weekends; the psychologist psychoanalyzes everything her husband says and does; we lose sleep over ongoing office troubles, or neglect to exercise in the rush of 12-hour work days. In ways big and small, we hurt ourselves and those around us by failing to draw the required lines around our work.

Of course, our work can suffer too if we fail to draw the appropriate lines. We start taking too many personal calls, or lose productivity when we spend our days talking to our colleagues about our personal lives.

Drawing appropriate lines and maintaining a healthy balance in our lives would be much easier if we all realized that we are not super human. We are not able to work 18 hours a day, plus have quality family time, plus contribute to the world around us, plus write that novel we have been dreaming of for years, plus... We have limits. We are each constrained by our abilities, our energies, and our environment. We cannot do all we would like to do. And that is a good thing. For while we strive in vain to do so much, we miss the possibility found *in doing what we can.*

Setting limits is key to liberating ourselves in the midst of life and work. It is much like the virtue of integrity, the oneness that holds us together. Call it the virtue of *clarity*, the virtue of knowing who and where we *are*, and who and where we *are not.* With clarity about these things, we can move back and forth from work to home and function healthily in both places.

But here is the second paradox. *Though there are some genuine differences between work and the rest of life, and though we need to set some clear limits between the two, our work and the rest of our lives share some real similarities.* To get to this point, though, we may need to change some of our ideas about home.

North American society has enforced a particularly romantic and consumer-oriented picture of home life and recreation or leisure. To our detriment, we associate home life with consumption. Work produces, and the rest of life consumes.

This vision of home life, as we saw in chapter two, greatly diminishes the value we place on work done in the home and on the people who do this work. It carries the implication that the work done *outside* the home, and those who do it, are what is really important, since it is *this* work and *these* people who bring the wealth, the luxury. Raising the kids, cleaning the house, doing the laundry, are all less important since they do not directly contribute to this wealth. In fact, the work done inside the home can even be *resented*, since it *consumes* so much of the wealth that has been created elsewhere.

Yes, home is a place of rest, and of recreation, and yes, both of those are consumptive activities. But home is *also* about *family* and *growth*, about *birth* and *death*. The work we do on those things requires discipline and energy. In and through them, we produce and become better people. Home, in other words, is a workplace – a place where we work on everything that really counts in an ultimate sense.

With this in mind, we can be free to take up the tasks of home with more energy. Taking out the garbage becomes just as important as doing the filing, and raising children even *more* important than strategic planning. Of course we do not always approach *any* of these tasks – either the ones we do at work or the ones we do at home – with delight, but we can begin to approach those we do in the home with the sense of value we usually reserve for work done outside the home.

Finally, and most importantly, a third paradox. *As we strive to take care of ourselves and to become whole, we need to give up a little on the self.* We need to be prepared to give up some of our dreams and aspirations, and to learn to live generously. Real life involves compromise, giving way, accepting less than we desire, and sometimes less than we need. That is what it takes to build relationships, to grow as communities, and to experience well-being as people in partnership with the universe.

It is also what we must do to find ourselves. When we push along a strictly self-centered and self-directed course, we become fundamentally lost. The key word is "fundamentally." We are not fundamentally *rational* and *linear* beings. Nor are we *complete*. Inside we are frazzled and frayed, mixed up and hopeful, wanting and needing others to provide balance and perspective. Following our own path, we stray outside the community which gives us perspective and balance. Eventually, we end up lost in a world of our own making, unattached to community, unable to see right and wrong, confused about what is truly important. It is in the process of working *with* and *for* each other that we grow, learn, and let go of self-involved confusion until we come close to the heart of ourselves and others. In the struggle to balance our own interests or to cast them in a larger framework, we become our true selves.

I do not say this lightly. I enjoy being able to say, "I did it my way." And yet, in all honesty, I know I have grown most as a person when I have let go of my aspirations and moved with the opportunities and needs presented to me. In situations which often seemed like detours, I found freedom and room to grow. Ironically, I also enjoyed these times more than most and experienced high levels of appreciation from others and great personal pride in accomplishment.

So what about all that talk, in chapter four, of following our interests, goals, and values? Clearly my career path has been shaped by my goals, my personality, and my particular set of personal and intellectual drives. But just as much, my accomplishments have been greatest when I was willing to put my own aspirations and plans to one side and to work in unfamiliar contexts. By going where *others* have asked me to go, I have come to see new sides to myself – powerful, positive, world-creating sides.

Family

In my experience, nothing clashes with work more than family. Both family and work are connected to our deepest identity issues and personal needs. Both demand time and attention. Both can make outrageous demands for loyalty. Many forms of work require that we be available 24 hours a day, and family *always* requires it. It is a huge and continuous tension.

It would be simpler if we could fix either one to an eight-hour-a-day time period. Many men have had that luxury, taking no responsibility for family matters that might come up while they were at work. Often, they extend that attitude to after hours as well. Some men still behave this way, though that pattern is changing as social expectations have changed, and as women have entered the workplace. Now most men – like nearly all women – have to cope with the demands of family as well as those of work.

At the same time, the home has become one of the locations of income-earning work. With technological advances, "home commuting" is a growing trend. Now many of us cannot leave our work by going home to the family; the work is there with us. Like it or not, the tension we experience between work and family is likely to grow.

The risk in this tension is that either one can damage the other. Work can destroy family, and family can destroy work. Women face the reality that if they choose to have a family, it may mean the derailment of a promising career. Many men give themselves so completely to their jobs that their families disintegrate. Both men and women frequently face the glare of co-workers, children and spouses as they try to balance competing needs. What do you do when you face a project deadline and your child, spouse, or parent is seriously ill? Children's sports and extra-curricular activities often call for one partner or the other to juggle a work schedule. Some people are blessed with flexible working conditions. But the pressure is still spectacular and can lead to major problems at home, or an inability to take on new responsibilities at work. The tension is real and for most of us unavoidable.

What makes this tension more complex is that work can often be used as an excuse to avoid, or a place to hide from family tensions. (In theory, it should work the other way too, that we could use family to avoid tensions at work. However, I suspect that any worker who routinely stayed home to avoid the stresses of work would soon – very soon – be out of a job.) If our teenagers are acting up, or if we are feeling pressured by our spouse, it can be very tempting to put in extra hours of work, or to take on an out-of-town project. To the degree that this avoidance "works," it reinforces itself. What may have started as a temporary measure – a short-term safety valve – can quickly become a habit. Many men have built a long pattern of family neglect, justifying their behavior with the claim that they *need* – as family provider – to work so hard.

The consequences can be, and have been, devastating. The family, of course, suffers. The teen does not get the attention he or she needs. Neither does the spouse. Eventually, the marriage may disintegrate. Conversely, the work situation can actually *improve* for the person who avoids their family in this way, since they will sometimes receive a pay increase or promotion in recognition of all their extra work. Success at work often masks problems at home.

Probably the best most of us can ever do to address the competing demands of work and family is to achieve some sort of dynamic balance, where what we "give" here is approximately balanced by what we "take" somewhere else, at some other time. We need to be flexible, able to move and shift and change the boundaries from time to time and still maintain the health of both sides. Flexibility involves knowing what is *essential*, what is perhaps *not so* essential, what is merely *peripheral*, and adjusting our actions appropriately.

We may be able to change peripheral things wildly, on the spur of the moment, without any damage. Who makes the kids' lunches today or who calls the baby-sitter to ask for an extra hour of time might be peripheral issues.

More important issues are changed less easily and usually require some intentional negotiation. These might include deciding who stays home with a sick child or who rearranges their schedule to retrieve the kids from hockey or ballet practice. (Other important issues include the division of labor – laundry, dish-washing, cleaning, grocery shopping, etc. – in the home.) The important thing will be to try to ensure that it is not always the same person who rearranges their work schedule or makes the concession. The issue here is one of fairness, as well as the potential threat to job security for the partner who most frequently needs to leave work to attend to family matters.

Essential issues or commitments such as a death or serious medical or emotional crisis in the family really should not be open to negotiation; they should be inviolable. Time together every week or holidays together should always be maintained, short of a complete catastrophe at work. Essential work commitments such as meeting customer service deadlines or completing critical processes on time must also be maintained, and only essential family matters should be allowed to override them.

Unfortunately, in our desire to be flexible, family often gets pushed aside. It seems, in most cases, to be easier to adjust family to work than the other way around. In part, this is because changing family routines does not show the immediate damage that missing a deadline at work shows. Family members are also usually more forgiving than the boss or other colleagues – especially in single income households. But the damage still occurs and most of us need to stop every so often and assess where we are with regard to our families.

It also needs to be said that far too many employers have still not adjusted their expectations to meet the needs of healthy families and homes. Most bosses gained their position at a time when loyalty to work was expected to exceed loyalty to family and they are still deeply entrenched in that way of thinking. *They* made sacrifices and they expect everyone else to make them too. This should no longer be acceptable and calls for *resistance* through confrontation. Family must come first. Home and health call for a revised set of priorities. Those who refuse to act accordingly need to be challenged.

The idea of confronting employers is not as far-fetched as it may first sound. In her book *Family* (Northstone, 1997), Betty Jane Wylie issues a similar "call to arms" and also suggests why this kind of confrontation does not happen more often. Although she is speaking specifically about the need to press for more daycare, what she say is, I think, generally applicable:

More and more parents are choosing not to destroy their personal lives. The idea of sacrificing their children to their jobs is increasingly repugnant ... Most parents haven't yet dug in their heels and rebelled in enough numbers to make their priorities clear ... Every family considers its own case so individual and personal that every time they hit a crisis parents think they're making a unique, one-time choice. They keep juggling their own lives and the lives of their children without realizing that others are doing the same thing. Again, it's a matter of getting priorities straight and then of realizing that there is bargaining strength in numbers.

In other words, there is much to be gained by confrontation. And yes, there is still much to be lost. Before you confront, be sure that your perspective is shared by those you work with.

Finally, remember to savor the good moments with family. Memories provide great encouragement. We will never resolve all the tensions, but we can find relative success and a measure of happiness if we give and take, are willing to settle for less than the ideal, and savor those times when it all works right.

Education for a Whole Life

Education is essential for our overall well-being, but it is especially so in the emerging workplace. This time in history is being called the information age, but it might be better called the age of knowledge. The term *information* tends to focus our attention on raw data. But information is only useful when it becomes knowledge: data processed by people and given a place or context. David Shenk has made this same point in his book *Data Smog* (Harper San Francisco, 1997): "Every day, more than 1,000 books are published and nearly 20 million words of technical data are recorded. It would take a reader eight hours a day for five months to consume just one day's output of the technical data." Shenk believes, as I do, that while people may be receiving more *information* in the Information Age, they're actually gaining less *knowledge* than before. Our information age requires "knowledge" and "*knowlegeable*" workers.

Usually, we process information into knowledge in two steps. The first step is an ongoing intake of information. We must look for new information, new bits and pieces which interest us or may be useful to us. The second step is education, learning to see how things are connected, how to relate one thing to another. Being a knowledgeable worker means being a perpetual student.

The willingness to study is a virtue. All of us should be taking courses, whether through the continuing education department of a local college or technical institute, a consulting group downtown, a retreat center that offers summer workshops, a school offering correspondence courses, or the Internet. There are thousands of courses out there on subjects ranging from basket weaving to Internet security. Taking a course exercises your mind in a disciplined way.

It helps if some of this learning is primarily theoretical. Technical knowledge, while important, must have a good theoretical basis to be useful to us today because it is often out of date before the textbook is printed. When we learn theory, we gain a frame of reference big enough to allow us to adjust and keep up. The social sciences – anthropology, sociology, psychology – all provide theory and insight into society and culture, and along with the liberal arts – philosophy, literature, rhetoric, history, and religion – train the student to think critically. We need to study things that shake us up and keep us open to new ideas.

I recommend taking at least one course per year in something fun and interesting, and maintaining at least one subscription to a magazine related to our field of work. Between the two, we will be pushed to understand more and better.

I said a bit ago that there were two steps involved in processing information into knowledge. I would now like to suggest a third step we can take. Once we have obtained knowledge, we should prepare to give it away. It has long been said that power not used is power lost. This also holds true for knowledge. Knowledge is fleeting and those who do not use it very quickly lose it. This is not because they no longer know things, but because the world has moved on and what was useful knowledge has now become outdated, though perhaps still interesting, trivia. Those with a strong capitalistic bent might conclude that knowledge obtained should quickly be sold. While I would agree in part – because that is the essence of much of today's *work* – I think many of us have obtained more knowledge than we can sell.

I suggest that once we have learned something useful, we should tell it to someone else who can use it. Put it in a memo, teach a course, tell your children, talk to a colleague over a cup of coffee. Put it into a simple and useful form and get the word out.

Giving knowledge away is the way of wisdom for anyone who wishes to lead. It is a gentle and generous way to power. We are all short on knowledge these days, and those who provide it quickly become important in our lives.

Finally, one of the greatest reasons to pursue education as part of our search for wholeness is because study opens the door to serendipity. Things learned in one place often apply in completely different places. The history of invention is filled with people looking for one thing and finding another. We are non-linear people living in a non-linear world, and so a wandering path is perhaps the surest course. We need to keep exploring if we, and the world around us, are to reach our full potential.

In my own experience, I have found that my background in church ministry has prepared me for the business world in ways I never expected. In fact, I would rank a Master of Divinity degree up there with a Master of Business Administration for relevance to the business world, particularly when it comes to working with highly complex situations, motivating people to excel, or being able to understand the social aspects of a problem. In other words, I never set out to become a business person, but the serendipitous possibilities which my path has created are at times wonderful to behold. Those same possibilities are open to *everyone* who follows the path of education.

Recreation and Rest

The relationship between recreation and work is a complex one. Usually we think of them as opposites. We work to earn the money that will allow us to do the recreational things we enjoy. We need one for the other. And, we think, we *enjoy* one more than the other.

We tend to think of rest and recreation as the ultimate goal of our working lives. Many of us enjoy travel, holidays, taking part in sports, hobbies and crafts, rest and relaxation. We look forward to retiring with enough financial security to allow us to do these things until we die.

But for few of us is this the real story. It rings true until it actually happens. Just ask someone who has been retired long enough to have moved past the first blush of excitement. Or someone who has suddenly become wealthy. Having spent years in productive labor, we find too much rest and recreation a terrible experience. Someone once defined hell as "getting what you want" and, indeed, the emptiness of recreation as an end in itself drives many to despair. Once we actually get it, the opportunity to spend our lives slouched in front of a TV or perpetually stuck on the golf links becomes a trap.

I do not mean to imply that recreation and rest are not important. They are very important. But they are not the point of life.

Most of us are looking for balance. We want movement between production and consumption, between work and rest. We are not happy with either one by itself. We need to find time to rest from our work, to re-create ourselves. At the same time, we need to go back to work to fulfill our urge to be productive participants in the world.

The difficulty lies in finding the right rhythm. We cannot depend on the seasons or the patterns of our work to provide it. To find the right balance of recreation and work, we must be attuned to the needs of our bodies, our work, and our communities. Each of these plays a vital role in signaling the right times for recreation and work.

All work drains us of energy. Our bodies wind down and give out as we work. It can happen quickly or slowly, our exhaustion can be physical or mental. Regardless, our work takes something out of us and so we need to take breaks. This does not mean that all of us will follow or need the same pattern of work and recreation. Each of us must be sensitive to those areas where and times when we are wearing out.

I know that after a long period of strenuous work I begin to feel crabby. I get irritated more easily with everyone, at home and at work. If I keep pushing, I get cold symptoms, such as a sore throat or a sinus headache. If I push further still, I find myself with a full-blown cold, often so bad that I lose a day or two of work. This generally happens to me once or twice a year. One of those times is often just before I take a vacation break. Because I know a vacation is coming soon, I ignore the signs that I need a break *now*, believing that I can wait. Typically I cannot, and so I get sick.

The fact that we wear out regardless of the type of work we do also means that we need to attend, in our rest and recreation, to the parts of our lives which may not get the attention they deserve at work. For office workers that usually means physical fitness. With busy schedules, sedentary jobs, and few obvious physical demands placed on us, we let ourselves become unfit. That means that our recreational activity should incorporate elements of physical exercise. We need to walk, run, or swim on a regular basis. These things become an essential part of self-care, for wellness in all parts of our lives. We cannot be whole if our bodies are not well.

Likewise, if our jobs incorporate physical exercise but little intellectual stimulation, we need to attend to our *mental* fitness. Like everything else about us, our minds weaken if we do nothing to exercise them. Reading, engaging in intelligent conversation with friends, taking a course, doing the crossword puzzle are all excellent recreational activities that exercise our minds, help us to think more clearly, and build long-term mental health.

Of course, our recreational activities can also compensate in very profound ways for other deficiencies at work. We all have multiple talents, interests, and capabilities. Personally, I am drawn in at least three very different directions. One is problem-solving. I love to solve deep and complex organizational problems, ideally with a financial component. I also love art and creativity. My third love is for issues of meaning. Now problem solving tends to be a marketable skill, and it tends to be the basis of my most satisfying work. But my other interests find little expression "on the job" and so I allow these to bloom in my recreation. I take night and Internet classes in philosophy and theology, and I get out with my camera and take pictures. In this way I achieve a degree of balance in regard to these interests as well.

Finally, our recreational activities can lead us closer to our good work. Even if we feel trapped in work which is not right for us, we are usually able to explore a full range of desires and abilities in our recreational activities. As we play ball or knit a sweater, we engage those parts of ourselves we feel best about. Instinctively, we explore and develop our natural gifts and interests. Coaching the little league baseball team develops a wide range of management and organizational abilities. Knitting requires patience, a good eye for shape and design, a high level of fine motor control, and the ability to follow complex directions. These things tell us about the type of work which has the potential to engage us more fully, and the skills themselves are often easily transferable to the work setting.

Following this model, recreation begins to look more like work than we first imagined. Instead of being the opposite of work, or a means of escape from work, it becomes its own form of work – a disciplined, productive activity which makes us more effective and balanced people.

When we think about it, this should not really surprise us. Despite the notion that recreation represents "free time," we tend to *schedule* this "free time" carefully for the long term. Whether we build model aircraft, sew quilts, plant flowers and vegetables, play tennis, or downhill ski, we invest large amounts of time in our leisure activities, and we constantly strive to do them better. We *work* at our play, and we need to.

Ideally, we use recreation to create a life rhythm, a harmonious flow or movement that enhances our work and all other aspects of our lives. When we can achieve this harmonious flow, we release energy and creativity into all of our life, and we become more capable at all our tasks. Ultimately, we will move from our work to the other areas of our lives with satisfaction and direction, allowing each its own time and space.

9

A Spirituality of Work

———

There is a monastery not far from where I live. Within it, a community of monks devotes their lives to the work of study and prayer. It is not the easiest life. Possessions are few, the hours long, and the rewards hard to see. Every year novices come, intent on joining the fellowship. Few of them find the work compatible and stay. Those who *do* stay pass out of public life, rarely noticed by any but the families they have left behind. But for them, it is enough. Their work reaches beyond the mundane to the sacred; and the work itself is sacred.

According to these monks, the picture of work I have described to this point is like a still life painting of a pond where the artist has forgotten to paint the shore. For them, there are boundaries, ultimate boundaries, places where the ripples of our existence and of our work finally hit their limits. They point out that the journey to the heart of all things has a specific destination, and that some ways to get there are much better than others.

For them, that means work finds its ultimate meaning in the image of Jesus Christ, the source of their community. They know their work to be sacred, because it takes them closer to the One who for them stands with welcoming (and wounded) arms at the heart of all things. Regardless of the tedium, endurance, or discipline involved, their work gives them joy because it is work at the boundaries, work where the ripples reach the shore.

Not all of us share their vision of the universe. There are even those who believe there is *no* fixed heart to the universe, but that the journey itself is what is important. Yet regardless of our stance, what these monks point out is true: there is work within the world, the type of work we have looked at to this point, and there is also work which focuses on the meaning of the journey. Two types of work, and we cannot ignore either in our exploration of good work.

The kind of work the monks do, work which focuses on the *meaning* of the journey, is not simple work. Nor is it easy. There is nothing about the ultimate that is either simple or easy. The words which describe this work are mysterious, disciplined, ambiguous, grace filled, hopeful, compassionate, dark, light, sublime, patient, and empty. They are words that come from the stories we tell of the way of all things, the images by means of which we understand this universe. They are words which create a task so demanding there are few who can achieve it, except those we call "holy": Jesus, the Buddha, the Prophet. Even then we recognize that the words we use are inadequate to describe where these holy wanderers have gone and what they have done, and that ultimately the words themselves are empty. Following these words is the work of the monks. They follow them down the long, hard path to the point of emptiness, and find in them, holiness.

At one time, it was enough that there were monks doing this work. The monks would pass their knowledge on to the religious leaders, who would pass it on to the civil leaders, and both would require it of the common people. This is not that time and we can no longer leave this work to the monks. In our world, where there are no clear answers, and there is no one we completely trust to teach us the "way of all things," each of us must also attempt to make this journey.

We cannot safely ignore this work and simply send our ripples out into the unknown. As we go about our day-to-day work, we change things from what they *are*, to what they *will be*. Because of this, we have a responsibility to have a sense of the ultimate direction of our work – whether it is toward good or toward ill. The work of the monks belongs to all of us – is *required* of all of us.

"Attending"

Though they do not put it in precisely these terms, the work of the monks is "attending." They "attend" to the universe, in its truest form. They listen and care for the most basic structures of reality. Just as eco-activists commit themselves to the work of caring for the physical network of life on the planet, the monks commit themselves to the work of caring for the *spiritual* network of life on the planet. Just as our physical world needs care and attention, they believe the spiritual world needs care and attention.

We forget this far too often, even though we may be able to *see* the spiritual side of things. But that, they say, is the same as admiring the view of a mountain while ignoring that others are strip-mining it away. Every act, by every person, either builds up or wears away the spiritual reality within which we live. The monks work hard, day after day, to build this world up. Without the *kind* of work they and others do, we lose sight of the ultimates and lose track of our fundamental stories. We become mired in the mundane and closed to the great mysterium that trembles just out of reach.

Good work requires that we do not neglect that which transcends. If we do not attend, as do the monks, we slowly lose sight of what is good. When we *do* attend, we are strengthened in our understanding and ability to cope with the shadowed side of our work and world. When we attend to the fundamentals, we become clearer about what it is that we are called to do.

I realize that this belief reflects a particular vision of the universe. But unless you believe that it is merely the mindless working of the laws of physics that governs all reality, then you will have to face something akin to what I suggest. If we believe in something greater than the details of our lives, then we must attend to it or risk losing all sight of it.

There are many ways to attend. The monks represent an extreme. Their particular monastery is cloistered away from the world. In their mountaintop retreat, they worship, pray, and teach. Thousands of people come to them to join them in worship, to learn from them what it means to attend. But most come down off the mountain at the end of the day and go back to more mundane ways of attending. For many who do not choose this mountaintop way, there are other communities of faith, each with its own way of attending. Other people seek to attend by becoming closer to nature. And still others by reading and reflecting on the journeys of the spiritual masters. There is no universal way to attend to the great realities.

This means that we must each seek to find a compatible community with whom we can learn to attend. For some of us this is easy. We join a gathering, learn from it, and "attend" with them. Others never find a permanent community with whom to do this work. Instead, they take from many, and create their own way.

Rules of "Attending"

However, there are rules to all forms of attending.

REGULARITY

The first rule is that of regularity. If we do not attend regularly, ideally daily, but at least weekly, we soon forget to attend at all. We all seem to need some time of regular quiet, a time we rigorously put aside simply for attending.

SILENCE

The second rule is silence, or at least quiet. Attending is best, though not always, done in the context of inner and outer silence.

FOCUS

The third rule is focus. Words and images help us trace the path to the ultimate. While there are imageless paths, they tend to be extremely difficult. Scriptures, candles, saints, and mandalas are all useful.

COMMUNITY

The fourth rule is community. This is not an easy rule to explain in our individualistic world, but I am tempted to add that unless you attend in the context of a community it is better not to attend at all. To ensure the integrity of the process, we need the assistance of those who can help us see the difference between our own minds and the ultimate reality to which we seek to attend.

These four rules are not easy to apply and that explains one of the reasons we do so little attending. It is hard, in our fast-paced, individualistic world to set time aside regularly, to find silence amidst the clamor of phones and family, to find a focus that works for us, and to find an appropriately insightful and supportive community.

However, if we *do* take on the discipline of attending, the rewards are great. Our day-to-day work will find new meaning and place in our lives. We will have new enthusiasm and energy. We will see more clearly and work more effectively. At the same time, we will understand better the way of all things, and become better people than we were before.

Vision

However, a caution. Attending, for the monks and for others who are spiritually mature, involves more than a body of *techniques*. To properly attend requires a vision. For the monks on the mountain, it is the vision of Jesus Christ. In that man, they find the center. He is the focus of their prayer and worship. It is from him, not from the techniques, that they gain their motivation and insight. It is *from* him that they gain their strength and *through* him that they deal with the obstacles they face in the work of attending. Once again, to attend requires a vision.

Where we will look for the vision necessary to guide this work is a choice each of us must make as adults. As children, most of us were raised according to some vision of the universe and our place and meaning within it. As adults with experience, we can continue to hold that vision, or we can choose to live by a different one. We can make something of our lives other than what we were given. Either way, once we have chosen this place, this vision, we must take the next step; we must integrate it with our work and the rest of our lives. A vision of the ultimate either has a meaningful connection to every detail of our lives, or it is not an ultimate vision. That means that the way we tell the story of how things "really are" has an impact on *everything* – on our work, our family, our sexuality, what we buy, what we do, the words we speak...

An Example: the Biblical Vision

One vision of the universe is found in Jewish and Christian scriptures. While this vision is not universally held, it has profoundly shaped Western culture and has had a tremendous impact on this book. I do not claim this vision to be absolute, or that it should not be open to changing interpretation – it has often, in fact, been reinterpreted by the very people who call it holy. Regardless, it is an extraordinary vision that, as illuminative example, can help us explore the way ultimate visions and work come together.

This Jewish and Christian vision of the universe begins with a story. It is a story that claims to place the pieces of life in their best order. In keeping with the ways of thinking of those who drafted the story, it is set at the beginning of time.

In this story, God created *everything* in the best way possible. The fundamental nature of reality was "good." Human beings were assigned a role in this new world; they were to be its gardeners, its caretakers, its stewards. But they were so taken with their power that they messed up. They did what they *wanted*, not what was *right*. This had consequences: they ruined the world permanently. Nothing was good, or as good as it had been, any longer. Where once humans *labored* in a lush garden that provided all they needed, now they *toiled* and existed only by the sweat of their brow. Relationships, too, went sour – brother turned against brother, tribe turned against tribe, every person turned against every other person.

The rest of Jewish and Christian scripture is about how to move things back toward some sort of equilibrium. Scripture, synagogue, and church are about how to restore some of that original "goodness." As suits any sacred story, it is highly complex, full of advances and reversals, insight and confusion, hope and despair. And ultimately it has no end.

Through this story we gain a vision for every part of our own lives. Nothing is left untouched, not even work. Through this story we can glimpse the true meaning of work itself, and clues to the type of work which will take us to the heart of all things.

Work itself, in this story, is honorable. But notice, it is more than that. In contrast to other stories of the universe where work is less than honorable (the ancient Greek, for instance), work, in this story, belongs to the inmost heart of things. It belongs to the *way* of all things. Work is what humans are *intended* to do in the very design of the universe. We do not work because we are *forced* to; we work because it is what we were *created* to do.

This story says something else. It says that all work takes into itself something of *holiness*. Whenever we work, we partake of something built into the most central fabric of the universe, and become holier, thereby. This is not a vision of a wealthy, holy priesthood. It is not the story of a royal family. It is a vision of ordinary people, doing ordinary work, but who are God's people nonetheless.

That is not all the story tells us. The tone of the story turns because the gardeners harvest that which is not to be harvested, and so bring the garden to an end. In other words, their work leads them to misclassify good and evil, and so to stray permanently from their calling. Just because *to work* is good does not mean that all things associated with it are good.

We could probe further and find more, but this is enough for now. This Jewish and Christian vision of the universe tells those who live by it two very important things about work. First, work is part of an original holiness. To do work is to enter holiness. Second, work can be wrong.

These two concepts extend the meaning of work as we have encountered it to this point. Earlier we saw that work was one of the ways we transform the stuff of the universe. This creation story adds two things to this insight. First, that this ability to transform is inherent in what it means to be human. We cannot run away from the power of transformation. Instead we must accept it, welcome it, and live by it. Not only do *we* transform, we must *be transformed*. At the same time, it adds a second insight: this power can indeed lead in deeply destructive directions. Not all work is good, and we can make terribly wrong choices, choices from which we and the planet may never recover. The corollary to this is that we can work right. There is a right work, or a right way of working, one that moves us and the universe along its appointed path.

In other words, the story pushes us to question the means and forms of our work. We *do* need to make decisions about which work is right, because this story indicates that not all work is necessarily so.

Practical Insights

These are very practical insights. Earlier in the book we looked at career choices. At that point we asked which was the right work for us. Now we must ask not only if a career choice is right for us, but also, is it right for the universe? Does it fit this vision of human life as caught between purpose and reality? Clearly, our work, according to this vision, should at least be in keeping with the type of world God created. Our career should have as its goal the maintaining or recreating of the world God intended. The marks of this "original" world were peace, plenty, and human beings living in close relationship with each other and the Earth. Any career which helps to create this type of situation will be more "fitting" than any work that does not. There is now a moral value to some careers and job choices which is not there for others. This story would logically lead us to place a high value on work that contributes to the care and development of others, or that manages Earth's resources in a responsible way so that the needs of *all* people *and* the needs of the environment itself can be met. In other words, this story advocates work that builds our human capacity to love and care for each other, or that heals and restores health to our relationships with each other and the Earth. Such work would be good work in its most ultimate sense.

Reengineering takes a new emphasis from this story. Now the goal is a little sharper and the need more intense. Not only can we go wrong, we can go *very* wrong, and the goal of reengineering in this light becomes that of ensuring that we reshape our work processes to reflect the aims of this story. It becomes important that we seek out work that is not right, work that violates this foundational story, and change it. Reengineering is a moral good of the highest order, one that holds the potential to re-create work.

These are only two examples, but you can see the way this story extends our understanding of work. This Jewish and Christian story has an impact on work and what we make of it. Those who live by this story will move in slightly different directions than those who do not, or those who do, but who interpret the story differently than I have.

Other Visions

Other visions – Marxist, Hindu, or feminist, for example – will extend the meaning of work in other directions. A Marxist would extend the meaning of work through its form of economic relations. The question of *who* is rewarded for *what* work is the new extension, and work that rewards *all* will be that which is most moral. Hindus will extend the meaning of work through the concept of Karma, seeing the highest morality in complete obedience to an individual's place in life (and the corresponding work). Feminists have extended the meaning of work by highlighting the relationships between the sexes, and moral work for them is that which does not discriminate along lines of gender.

Each vision of the foundational order of the universe will extend the understanding of work in a different direction. Some of these visions may be compatible with one another – for example, the Christian and feminist visions – while others may be contradictory. Regardless, no matter how we imagine the shape and meaning of the universe, it will change the way we understand work.

Working Responsibly

This leaves us with a great responsibility. Our knowledge of what we are doing when we work puts on our shoulders the responsibility to make good choices and to do our best to see that the world becomes a better place. Our work changes the world, and this is no small thing. In fact, it cuts to the heart of everything. Those who carry this knowledge are required to live and work out of it.

Regardless of the specific vision of the universe we may hold, we have been *given* life and we are now responsible for *giving* life. Each of us has been gifted with life itself, and *through* life the opportunity to shape and reshape the world. In our hands lies the power to create or destroy, to build up or tear down, to enhance or detract. To accept the gift of life is to accept the responsibility of *creating*, so that future generations may know life, and know it as *gift*.

This means that our work must give life to the world. Responsible work takes the stuff of our existence and shapes it to produce a new world where all creatures can live, grow, reproduce, experiment, and create with greater freedom and better direction than they could before our work. Life after our work should have new potential, new vibrancy, new hope, and new opportunity. We should be able, at the end of our work, to say, "It is good."

This is a call to action that demands the application of the best of our ability, a lifelong commitment to learning, and the development of great discipline. It is, in fact, a responsibility that demands everything we have to give. We are challenged to see in our work a lifelong calling. We are challenged to see in our work the opportunity of a lifetime. Our work is very serious business. It is up to us to create the world we and future generations will want to live in.

If there was only one possible vision of how things should be, or if the universe was susceptible to rational analysis, our task might be easier. Instead we have to make our own way, as individuals and communities, and this means making decisions which will always be relative in their adequacy. We do not know enough to make perfect decisions. We can only do the best we can in any given situation. We must regularly choose the best option from a limited range of options, a range that is narrower than it should be. As well, even within a limited range of options, we cannot always predict the outcomes of our actions. This is why we must always strive to know more about the outcomes of our work, and to increase our range of options. Our task is difficult because there is never clarity.

The good news is that whenever we strive to do the best we can do, to *be* the best we can be, our efforts are multiplied, seemingly by the universe itself, and our good work ripples out in growing waves. Our limited efforts have an impact out of all proportion to our ability. The best we can do is *all* we can do, and it seems to be good enough. If we *strive* for the best, we get closer than at first seems possible.

Journey Positively

We must also realize that this responsibility encompasses not only the goal toward which we work, the destination toward which we journey, but also the *way* we journey. There are many ways of traveling, and not all of them are consistent with the destination. Our way of moving toward life must itself be lively.

Since our journey is toward life, it must be marked *by* life. We must proceed *joyfully*, celebrating whenever a celebration is appropriate. We must proceed *cooperatively*, so that others may join us. We must proceed *hopefully*, so that no one gives up. And we must proceed *(pro)creatively* so that the path is marked with *new* life. The *way* of our journey lends much to its eventual outcome.

When I set out to climb a mountain, I must take pleasure in the climbing and celebrate the view along the way. Failure to do so leads to a grimness of spirit which will haunt the path, no matter how accomplished a "climber" I may be. It also leads to isolation. I am unlikely to find too many companions to join me if I proceed only by grim determination. If we wish to climb with others, we must climb in such a way as to use every step and every handhold as a new opportunity to enjoy, celebrate, and learn.

Hold Things Lightly

The journey holds one last challenge, however, for those who come this far. This challenge exists because life complicates even the best of plans and processes. Life is inherently unstable, interruptive, eruptive, evocative, and allusive. While we try to set a straight-line course and ensure that we walk it correctly, life is busy sliding sideways into new forms and shapes. New things, ideas, and events bubble up unbidden. As a result, our journey will be filled with irony and surprise.

Because of this, we must *hold things lightly* if we wish to hold them at all. We must let the potential in each situation emerge, treat each moment with the respect it is due, and remain open to new things.

For those who journey joyfully and in the company of others, the ability to hold things lightly is a lesson quickly learned. In the pleasure of the moment and in the give and take of camaraderie, it is easy to let go of that which no longer fits. Like children on a beach, we find so much potential in each new discovery, we move expectantly and without regret from one thing to the next.

In work as in life, every moment is shrouded in mystery before it happens, veiled in potential, screened by possibilities. And so we must work hard, the best we can, and be prepared to be surprised. Good work is a never-ending adventure.